Contents

Preface

The origins of this book are to be found in my experience of teaching introductory sociology to first-year university students. Increasingly, I have found this means addressing a very heterogeneous group of students. Some of them have never encountered sociology before, while some of them have already had as much as four years of sociology as part of their secondary education. Many of them, what's more, are simply picking up a bit of sociology as part of a wider first-year menu and have little or no interest in taking the subject further or indeed taking it particularly seriously.

Diversity of this order is challenging. It means that there are even more difficult choices than usual to be made about what and how to teach. For example, adopting a historical 'who said what' approach, or basing the course in the 'great schools of thought', would be likely to replicate much of the school sociology curriculum and alienate half the audience. I'd also find it pretty unrewarding personally: sociology isn't primarily about sociologists – whether living or dead, black or white, female or male – and what they've said. Sociology is about the world of humans and how we are to understand it. However, simply launching into a survey of the substantive sociology of this or that aspect of the human world would be to take for granted too many necessary preliminaries and run the risk of mystifying the other half of the audience. Despite the availability of some really excellent introductory teaching materials, finding a strategy that works isn't easy.

In attempting to introduce complete novices to the ways in which sociology can enhance their understanding of their own lives – and it's one of the firmest presumptions of this book that it can – while at the same time offering more knowledgeable students something sufficiently interesting and challenging, I opted to return to basics: to the nature of sociology as a systematic investigative activity and, even more important perhaps, to the nature of its subject matter. This latter, in particular, demanded that I identify, amid the contemporary proliferation of sociological themes and approaches, what I believed to be the fundamental themes and concerns of the discipline. Having done so – which wasn't always easy, because these bedrock concepts and questions are largely taken-for-granted in everyday sociology – the job in hand demanded that I critically re-assess their usefulness and value.

Probably unsurprisingly, this turned out not to be as straightforward as I'd imagined. An audience of several hundred students has a wonderful way of concentrating the mind, and in the course of several years examining the axiomatic presumptions of the discipline I came slowly to believe that some of our most fundamental concepts and approaches don't actually help us to understand the human world. Quite the reverse. On close inspection, these sociological foundations – concepts as basic to the sociological enterprise as 'society' or 'culture' – are distinctly rickety. To stay with the metaphor, they need to be shored up in places, re-built in others, and sometimes re-dug in a different location or direction altogether. There are other foundations, too – in particular those which underpin our collective empirical responsibilities – which seem to have become overgrown with the creeping and choking intellectual foliage of a century or more of sociological expansion and disagreement. The sociological propensity for regular, and non-cumulative, re-invention of the wheel has been a particular problem in this respect. In the interests of clarification, if nothing else, some pruning of the undergrowth is in order.

Despite its origins, therefore, this book is not in any obvious sense an 'introduction to sociology'. Although it is an overview of some very basic issues, and is addressed to an intended readership which includes students, a certain amount of knowledge is necessarily assumed. What began as a set of first-year sociology lectures has evolved gradually into an argument which is intended to re-orient the discipline's point of view on its subject matter.

Furthermore, although this is unmistakably a 'theory book', it is not *about* theory as such: I am only concerned with theorists in so far as they shed light on the matter in hand. This book is about the human world first, and how, as a discipline called sociology, we can understand that world, second.

That the book's goals might be seen as ambitious does not, however, mean that I make any claims to startling originality. To reiterate my earlier point about the re-invention of the wheel, the concepts and methods that we need, if we are to approach and understand the human world in the manner which I am suggesting, have been available to us in one shape or another for quite a long time. During the 1990s the pursuit of novelty became a blight on much of what passes for sociology, so no matter how this book is received it isn't offered as a dramatically new departure.

On the other hand, however, I do not mean to appeal to a sense of traditionalism either. The project in which I am engaged isn't that kind of 'back to basics'. While the themes and lines of thought that I am exploring have regularly been articulated here and there throughout sociology's first century, they have typically been a minority voice, attracting little cumulative attention or following. There is, thank goodness, no 'tradition' to which to return.

Every book is the product of a long process, involving others than the author. Since the intellectual wherewithal to write this book came from the experience of teaching, I must, before I acknowledge anyone else, thank my students over the years. I am particularly grateful to successive classes of Level One students in Sociological Studies at the University of Sheffield for their comments during conversations and seminars and, not least, the sharpness of some of their criticisms in written course evaluations.

Apropos teaching, I must thank Tracey Warren, my sometime colleague and partner in Level One crime at Sheffield, for bringing my introductory teaching to the attention of Catherine Gray, my editor at Palgrave Macmillan. Tracey saw the possibilities, and Catherine breathed life into the project, when I was very dubious about its likelihood and prospects. Catherine has encouraged and contributed to the work at every step, and for her detailed commentary, if nothing else, deserves much more than the customary author's thanks.

A number of other people have read all or part of the book and made helpful comments. In addition to the three anonymous publisher's readers – who did an exemplary job, and to whom I owe an enormous amount – Anne Henderson Bissenbakker, Jenny Owen, David Phillips, Vibeke Steffen, and Tracey Warren all deserve a mention and a thank you in this respect. Jenny Owen, who was an unfailing source of support and properly critical encouragement throughout, deserves a special final mention. No ordinary acknowledgement could be sufficient.

One
Foundations of Sociology

Criticism of sociology from within the discipline has a respectable pedigree. It may indeed be intrinsic to the enterprise. More than forty years ago, C. Wright Mills famously diagnosed sociology as suffering from confusion, distortion, bureaucratisation, and shoddy craftsmanship.[1] A decade or so later, Alvin Gouldner, no less famously, hailed a 'coming crisis' in sociology, arguing for a radical theoretical and political reflexivity appropriate to a historical moment – it was the end of the 1960s – when 'new sentiments and old theories' were out of kilter with each other.[2] At roughly the same time Stanislav Andreski fired off a barrage of broadsides aimed at everything from the obscure language of sociological writing, to the methodological pretensions of sociological research, to ideology masquerading as theory.[3]

For the next couple of decades, the critical heights were largely commanded by the big guns of feminism. The women said – and it was nearly all women, and they were right – that sociology was professionally élitist with respect to gender, intellectually élitist in many of its concerns and its style, and, perhaps most important, strikingly out of step with one of the most obvious and fundamental observable realities of the human world, that half the people in it were women, no less significant than the men.[4] Move on to the beginning of the twenty-first century and John Goldthorpe can be heard bemoaning the 'general, and steadily worsening disarray' of sociology,[5] as manifest in the lack of integration between research and theory, the collective failure of sociologists to decide what kind of discipline sociology should be, and disagreement as to whether this amounts to healthy pluralism or chaotic fragmentation.

1

Much of what these critics, and others,[6] have had to say over the years is defensible and important. In the cases of Mills and Andreski in particular, and the feminists in general, there is an enormous amount that, regrettably, continues to resonate loudly despite the passage of time. If I were writing in a similarly critical vein here, I would focus on three significant senses – which I'm not the first person to identify – in which contemporary sociology can and should be challenged:

- first, general theory and empirical research have become too weakly connected to each other;[7]
- second, sociologists routinely fail, at least in large part because of the ways in which they write, to address the wide audience that the discipline's subject matter surely demands;[8] and
- third, the sociological aspiration to objectivity – problematic as it is – which is so vital if we are to defend successfully our claims to understand the human world,[9] has been particularly threatened in recent years.

Although I will necessarily return to these points in what follows, they are not the main themes of this book. My key questions are in a different vein and point in a different direction:

- What is the distinctive realm of human experience and existence?
- How are we to understand that human world better?
- How can sociology contribute to that understanding?

At the risk of drawing too sharply distinctions which, as I will discuss later, are utterly fuzzy in sociological practice, the first question would conventionally be understood as broadly *ontological*, the second as *epistemological*, and the third as *methodological*. Before exploring them in detail in the rest of the book, it may be helpful to signpost some of the most important points of the argument and to offer some initial conceptual clarification.

Defining a Sociological Field of Vision

The 'human world', or the 'world of humans', is the distinctive realm of human experience and existence to which I have just referred, and the subject matter with which sociology as I understand it is concerned. The expression itself has an interesting personal history in that I thought for quite a while that I had arrived at it myself. I was pleased with it, and with myself: it's simple and uncomplicated, and, as I shall explain below, does a number of jobs well.

Imagine, therefore, the mild embarrassment – but also the pleasure and the reassurance of recognition – with which I recently re-read Zygmunt Bauman's wonderful *Thinking Sociologically*, to discover that its pages, and especially the introductory pages in which he is outlining the scope of sociology, are peppered with the same or similar expressions, beginning with 'the *human-made* world, . . . the part of the world, or the aspect of the world, that bears the imprint of human activity, that would not exist at all but for the actions of human beings'.[10] That's a reasonable definition of what I'm talking about here, and another reminder that not much of what I'm talking about is actually new.

So why choose this form of words to talk about what others might, for example, call the 'social world'? There are a number of closely-related good reasons. First, the concepts of 'society' and 'culture' – which often stand for the human-made world – have sufficiently serious limitations and shortcomings, which I will discuss in Chapter Three, to suggest that we might need a more robust alternative. Secondly, the notion of the 'human world' is self-evidently and unashamedly an anthropocentric perspective on the world. Real embodied humans are placed right at the heart of what sociology is interested in. This in turn means that humans' distinctive sphere of experience and power is evoked as a concrete, tangible, three-dimensional reality (which isn't to suggest that we don't need abstraction to talk about and understand it).

In the third place – and however we conceptualise it – that the 'human world' is necessarily filled with embodied humans means, no less necessarily, that they will be doing stuff, individually and in concert with other humans: they will be active and acting, acting upon and acted upon. Although this may seem to be an obvious point, like so much that appears to be obvious it can quickly fade from view if we cease to remind ourselves of it. As is illustrated by much of what Bryan Turner has recently called 'decorative theory',[11] out of sight very quickly becomes out of mind in this respect, and the activity and creativity of the human world and the humans who constitute it can dwindle and decline to a static structure or a passive text. The human world is more than just the object of our disciplinary gaze.

Fourthly, to talk about the human world is to take in individuality and collectivity as simultaneous aspects of one reality. While the notion of a 'world' necessarily evokes a space bigger than, and irreducible to, individuals, qualifying it as 'human' equally necessarily identifies active embodied human individuals as its key elements. It thus becomes more difficult to engage in what are, from the point of view that I am adopting throughout this book, essentially sterile arguments about which should be the real object of sociology's attention – the individual or the collective – and which one might be more important than, or determine, the other.

Taken together, these arguments in support of the notion of the 'human world' have the further merit of discouraging the temptation to reify the collective aspects of human life, which has always been such a problem for sociological theorising and which makes a significant contribution to the often distant relationship between general theory and systematic inquiry into the observable realities of the human world. In both of these respects, the 'human world' is a significant improvement on concepts such as 'society' or 'culture'.

Finally, to talk about the human world offers sociology further added value in that it permits a sociological recognition of the fact that human beings, in all of their complexity, are also organic beings. Specifically, the notion of the human world doesn't rest on those long-established ontological presumptions which distinguish 'culture' and 'society' from 'nature' – or 'the social' and 'the cultural' from 'the natural' – as different kinds of 'things'. Without wishing to anticipate it in detail here, an argument will be developed in Chapter Six which lays the foundations for incorporating into sociology an ecological understanding of the human world as an integral part of the natural world.

Ontology, Epistemology and Methodology

This brings me to the *ontology* of the human world. What does it consists of? What *is* it? These are disarmingly simple questions in the first instance. Bearing in mind the definition borrowed from Bauman, above, the human world is made up of organically embodied human individuals, their actions and practices, and their products. The latter includes everything from housing, to language, to domesticated animals, to music, to law, to nuclear submarines, to global warming.

This is all very obvious, and reassuringly material, but where does it leave collectivity, that sense of the more-than-the-sum-of-the-parts which I identify throughout this book as an enduring defining feature of the human world? Focusing on the actions and products of humans, there are *at least* five dimensions, each immediately apparent and substantial, to the ontology of the collective. Collective 'more-ness' is to be found in the following intimately connected features of the everyday human world:

- enchantment, the human refusal to accept physical appearances as the sum total of the human world, which is manifest in many aspects of everyday life, from religion to literature;
- the mutualities of group identification, the construction of membership on the basis of we-ness, inclusion, and similarity, on the one hand, and they-ness, exclusion, and difference, on the other;
- learned and shared symbolic universes, which include all the repertoires of verbal and non-verbal communication, as the foundations of intersubjectivity and knowledge;

- the qualitative geometry of social relationships, which ensures that when three people relate to each other the fundamental nature of the situation differs from when there are two participants; and
- the stabilisation of 'the present' as a collective working time-space, which provides humans with secure horizons within which to go about their daily lives.

I will discuss these further in Chapter Four. For the moment this list is sufficient to show that collectivity is far from being ineffable or empirically mysterious.

Talking about how we can perceive the collective more-than-the-sum-of-the-parts moves the discussion on to *epistemology*: how are we to know and understand the human world? Before answering that question it is necessary to clarify the relationship between ontology and epistemology. The basic point is that there is no sense in which one is, logically or otherwise, prior to the other. The distinction between what exists and how it can be known may in principle be clear, but the relationship between the two is intimate and necessarily two-way, meeting in our working notions of what can plausibly be *said* to exist and how that knowledge can be justified as plausible.

Adopting this point of view, and having argued for a bare ontology of what the human world amounts to, I will argue in Chapter Four that we can usefully understand the human world by adopting an analytical framework comprising three theoretical or classificatory orders: the individual, the interactional, and the institutional. These are not to be confused with the embodied human individuals mentioned above, their actions and practices, or their products. The individual, the interactional and the institutional *orders* do not exist in the way that individuals, interaction and institutions can be said to exist. They are simply 'ways of talking' about those realities, designed to help us to think about them, and the relationships between them, in a systematic fashion. In terms of observable reality, the three orders are simply different ways of looking at the same phenomena: the embodied individuals of the human world.

If ontology and epistemology are intimate bedfellows, they need to make room beside them for *methodology* too. Defined here as systematic applied epistemology (it could also, and no less sensibly, be called applied ontology), sociological methodology is concerned with which data-gathering procedures we should adopt – what we should *do* – in order to explore and understand the human world in a plausible and defensible fashion.[12] In sociological practice these conventional distinctions between ontology, epistemology and methodology are difficult to maintain, if only because explanation and method are utterly and reciprocally conditioned by how the nature of human phenomena is understood in the first place.[13] Reality assumptions about the human world inevitably imply judgements about how it is possible to know that world, and *vice versa*.

Be that as it may, methodology carries with it the very strong presumption that there is something to find out: that there are observable realities of and in the human world. Now it is possible that hackles may rise here, at my use of words such as 'real' and 'reality': that it is possible to know 'reality' is a notion with which some sociologists appear to have become uncomfortable, for a range of reasons which I will discuss in Chapter Five. Suffice it to say at this point that I think that it's possible to have too much epistemological sophistication. It's certainly possible to fret about such matters to the point where the only likely consequence is a failure of epistemological nerve and a retreat into the safety and luxury of pure theory.

To put this another way, doesn't everyone who does empirical research have some sense of the observable reality of the human world? Furthermore, aren't we all realists of a sort as we go about our daily lives? How, in fact, could it be otherwise? And if we can't conduct ourselves as everyday people without a sense of the reality of the human world, why should we conduct ourselves differently as sociologists? If there isn't something out there, about which it is possible to find something out with some confidence, and about which it is subsequently possible to say something more or less defensible, what *is* the point?

Whether in everyday life or as sociological researchers we need defensible, evidence-based generalisations which allow us to have reasonable, even if circumspect, expectations about what is more or less likely to happen in the immediate future. In this respect I am arguing for the adoption of an attitude towards the human world which can be called *everyday realism* – although either David Silverman's 'cautious positivism' or Gregor McLennan's 'positivity' might also do at a pinch[14] – to which we can own up and with which we can live comfortably.

Sociological Objectivity

Everyday realism carries with it a responsibility to document the observable realities of the human world as accurately as we can. Objectivity is one of the key issues in this respect. If we are to make any plausible claim at all to understand the human world, and if the understanding that we offer is to stand any chance of being accepted as non-partisan or unbiased, then it is vital that we make at least some attempt to be objective.

This issue has been a thorn in the collective sociological side for many years.[15] Emerging in part from a long-standing critical debate about Max Weber's original vision of a value-neutral sociology,[16] in part from an equally hoary set of disagreements about whether or not sociology can, or should, be considered a science – something to which I will return in Chapter Two – and in part from an insistence that the personal is also the political (in which case all knowledge claims are political), it has become something of a conventional sociological wisdom to assert that objectivity is a myth. In its strongest version, this standpoint welcomes explicit ideology and the pursuit of political objectives – as long as they are emancipatory political objectives, of course – as preferable to the dangerous delusion or deceit of claiming objectivity where none exists.[17]

I want to argue for a somewhat different standpoint. The aspiration to objectivity is not only important – we should be working towards it all the time, even if there's no utopia of absolute objectivity – but it's an aspiration which isn't wholly unrealistic. While this argument is obviously grounded in my earlier remarks about everyday realism and observable reality, it also derives from a belief that for a long time we seem to have been mixing up two rather different understandings of objectivity, one to do with our politics and values, the other with knowledge.

In the first of these senses, objectivity is probably more of a hindrance to sociology than a help. Do we really want to adopt an attitude to the human world of indifference or disinterest? Is it, indeed, possible? And can we afford to? Since it is, after all, our world, such a position would come perilously close to indifference towards ourselves. It would certainly call into question the point of doing sociology at all. Disinterested, value-free sociology – given that our driving wheel is, or should be, an interest in the doings and products of real, embodied human beings – is at best a contradiction in terms. The sociologist without politics or values, without an ethical point of view on the human world, sounds too much like Nietzsche's 'specialists without spirit' invoked by Weber at the end of *The Protestant Ethic*[18] for my liking.

But espousing a political or ethical point of view need not prevent us from striving towards objectivity in its second sense.[19] In fact, having a point of view positively demands that we should do so. If there is such a thing as observable reality – in other words, if the human world isn't simply in the eye of the beholder, a merry-go-round of different perceptions and representations, any one of which is as valid as any other – then, whatever our politics or values, and whatever the projects and goals that flow from them, nothing but the clearest and the most accurate observation of, and information about, that world will do. It's the difference between building on rock and building on sand.

This does not, for example, mean that we can see and understand the world unmediated by our language and concepts. It does not mean that the world is 'just there' and that we can apprehend its reality in some unproblematic fashion. What objectivity in this sense *does* mean is standing as far back as possible from whatever aspects of the world of humans are in our sights, in order to facilitate the clearest, most complete view possible. It means working hard to prevent politics and values getting in the way of finding out as *much* as we can, as *honestly* as we can, and as *systematically* as we can. A degree of hard-won critical distance is not the same thing as disinterest.

When Karl Marx argued, a century and a half ago, that understanding the world was for mere philosophers, and that the real point was to change it,[20] he laid the foundations of a confusion that continues to dog our attempts to understand the human world. Put simply, this involves mistaking how we would *like* the world to be, for how it actually *is*. Not only is there no necessary connection between these two things – to say which is not to deny the good sense of planning for desired outcomes on the basis of the best available evidence – but the latter frequently gets in the way of seeing the former. Allowing desired outcomes to determine the availability and acceptability of evidence is to put the ideological cart before the epistemo-logical and methodological horses. Facts can no more be derived from values than the other way round (which does not, however, mean that morality and knowledge are unconnected or irrelevant to each other).

While the natural sciences are far from immune, ideology is a particular pitfall when it comes to understanding the human world because we are actually part of that world: we are our own subject matter, albeit generally at a remove. It can thus be very difficult to prevent ourselves from seeing what *is* through the filter of what we believe *ought* to be, or what we *want*. While ideology's pervasive temptations are not restricted to sociology – the histories of psychology and economics, for example, are littered with the debris of ideological wishful thinking – this is no excuse for complacency. There are too many examples ready to hand for that, and their consequences are too debilitating intellectually.

For the purposes of illustration it may be helpful to consider briefly three of these. It is not so long ago – one only has to go back to the 1970s – that the argument that human behaviour was determined by economic and material circumstances, and human history determined by classes and class conflict, was thought to be interesting and important, politically and socio-logically.[21] As, in part, a generational battle-ground between self-styled radicals and conservatives, many of whom would have difficulty recognising that the term 'ideological' applied to them, these notions often produced some very bad-tempered encounters. Viewed from today, when class as a key concept is perhaps in need of some sociological rehabilitation, the debate looks futile and destructive. With the wisdom of hindsight, Marx's well-known disavowal that he was a Marxist may have been apposite here.

A more up-to-date example is the reluctance that many sociologists seem to have, when talking about sex and gender, to recognise that the observable realities of organic embodiment make a difference to the lives of men and women, and that this difference is sociologically relevant and interesting.[22] Since I discuss this matter further in Chapter Six, I will not expand on it here, other than to suggest that it offers an uncomfortable example of the ease with which awkward issues, instead of being investigated, are 'resolved' by becoming taken-for-granted background conventional wisdom. If nothing else, it makes for a quieter life.

Finally, it is worth pondering briefly the heat rather than light that is often generated by the concept of rational, calculative action. Personally, I find it difficult to actually believe that the more committed sociological protagonists in this argument can *really* think either of the two extreme options: (a) that rational calculation is the only sensible explanation of the patterns of human behaviour, or (b) that rational action explains nothing at all (and, what's more, is probably an illusion). Since this is, however, what they say,[23] I must take their word for it, despite the violence that either position does to the complexities of the human world.

Ideology is a particularly problematic barrier to our under-standing when it comes to the specification of fundamental, ontological properties of humans and the human world by ideological fiat, rather than on the basis of a more, dare I say it, *reasoned* consideration of the available evidence. All of the examples referred to immediately above demonstrate more than their fair share of this ideological tunnel vision. This is a particularly problematic issue for sociologists because, while the discipline may not be able to claim to be a science – and many of us wouldn't want to go down that road anyway – we do claim to be a rational discourse.

Our own ideologies aside, less high-minded considerations – to do with funding, usefulness and politics – also pose significant problems for objectivity. The social problem-driven agendas of funding agencies influence which empirical topics and problems are investigated, which questions are asked, and which methods are considered acceptable. Nor is this situation only a result of the economic difficulties of higher education, or the cynical individual pursuit of career advantage. There is an unforced affinity between the priorities and values of many sociologists, who genuinely want to be useful and to do good – and who can blame them? – and those of government departments, research councils, charities and foundations. There is also the continuing problem of sociology's shaky legitimacy. Why else do some of our most eminent still feel the need to produce books with titles such as *In Defence of Sociology*?[24] Our inability to be scientific, our basic uncertainties, and the persistent whiff of radical sulphur which we know still clings to sociology in many nostrils, may sometimes make us more anxious to please than we ought to be.

This isn't all bad news. Much good work is done under these constraints, and much of it, perhaps, because of them. Nor, as I have already argued, is it either possible or desirable to purge sociology of politics and values (particularly not compassion). But it is possible and desirable, always and under all circumstances, to aim for as much critical distance as possible from whatever it is we are researching, in order to allow ourselves the best possible prospect, and the clearest possible vision. The pursuit of this *epistemological* objectivity – even if the working outcome is only ever 'good enough objectivity' – is not something we should shy away from or deny. If sociology's claims to understand the human world are going to be taken seriously by the rest of that world, it's vital.

These then are some of the foundations of sociology with which I am concerned in this book:

- in respect of subject matter, a definition of our distinctive field of vision as 'the human world';
- an ontology of that human world which rests on the observable realities of individuals and collectivities;
- an understanding and analysis of that human world in terms of individual, interactional and institutional orders;
- a refusal to draw a sharp line between the human world and the natural world; and
- a standpoint towards the human world and the natural world based in everyday realism and epistemological objectivity.

There are two further foundational points to make here. The first harks back to my earlier criticism that sociologists routinely fail to address the broad popular audience that our subject matter – the human world – surely demands. This is partly a matter of intellectual democracy, and the role of sociology as critique, to which I will return in the closing chapter. On another tack, however, I want to raise the ante further and insist that we also have an *ethical* responsibility to address this problem. If nothing else, the people about whom we write deserve to be able to understand what we say about them better, and more easily, than they generally can at the moment. While discharging this responsibility is unlikely to prove easy or comfortable, I don't believe that the present sorry state of affairs is beyond redemption. Nor do I think that there is any need to 'dumb down': this carries with it an implication that the rest of the human world is dumb, which is as wrong as it is patronising and disrespectful.

The present book addresses this problem in two mutually reinforcing ways, the first of which concerns language. The scandal of sociology's 'barbaric dialect'[25] has been pointed out so often – and, depressingly, to such minimal effect – that it hardly needs to be discussed any more. I don't intend to labour the point here. Taking comfort from the example of authors such as George Ritzer and Richard Sennett,[26] suffice it to say that this whole book, and the style in which it's written, is offered as an illustration that it is possible to talk about subtle and complex sociological matters, and even to make a contribution to sociological theory, in language which is relatively lucid and accessible.

The second contribution that this book might make to improving the situation brings me back to the conceptual undergrowth which needs to be cut back if we are to perceive and understand the human world better. Once again, it's the book as a whole which is intended as a contribution in this respect rather than any specific part of my argument. In particular, I have consistently tried to recast the foundations which underpin the sociological worldview[27] in the least elaborate ways that I could find. While simplicity is not everything – both the human world and our audience would be poorly served by over-simplification – complexity which is a product of our concepts and style of presentation, rather than a feature of the observable realities with which we are concerned, is to be avoided.

My final point is about the meaning of the word 'sociology' and the nature of the discipline. Although sociology can for many mundane and defensible purposes be defined in narrow institutional terms – teaching departments, diplomas and degrees, syllabi and the like – I have in mind a broader vision: of an intellectual field and activity concerned to understand and investigate the human world in characteristic ways and from a characteristic point of view, taking in the traditions and methods of social anthropology, social history, and much social psychology, in addition to sociology. This intellectual enterprise – which I summarise here as *generic sociology*[28] – is the sociology to which the book's title refers and the subject of the next chapter.

Two
What is Sociology?

There are many views about what sociology is and what its business should be, all of them bound up with questions about the nature of its subject matter. Apart from the vague 'study of society' that's probably the most common fall-back position, sociology can be defined in a number of complementary ways. At its most basic it is the study of patterns in human behaviour. Among other things this means that sociology pays particular attention to established relationships between humans, which is why the study of institutions and how they work has always been fundamental to the sociological enterprise. Sociology has, however, always been as interested in individuals as in collectivities. It is particularly concerned with the many ways in which individuals are influenced by human factors outside their immediate environment or control. Finally, sociology has always been concerned with the shared ways in which human beings interpret their lives, with meaning.

What connects all of these is that sociology is the study of the recurrent or regular aspects of human behaviour. Wishing one neighbour a good morning and ignoring another is not, as a one-off occurrence, sociologically interesting. Do it every day, and, as an established relationship of inclusion and exclusion, it becomes so. If this can be connected to wider patterns of behaviour – for example, if the neighbour that you ignore is a member of a different ethnic group than both you and the neighbour that you greet – its sociological interest increases. Similarly, the fact that one woman is elected to an otherwise all-male legislature isn't necessarily sociologically significant. However, that women members come, over time, to number in their tens, scores or hundreds, certainly is.

However we define sociology's subject matter there will be many different perspectives on it. There are those for whom the fundamental building blocks of sociological analysis can only be individuals, others for whom they must be collectivities. Some sociologists believe we can establish the causes of human behaviour and its patterns, others insist that all we can do is interpret what people do. While some adopt a detached and apparently disinterested perspective on the human world, others think that sociology should be actively oriented towards intervention. Some base their understanding of the human world on numbers and quantity, others focus on in-depth description. There are many different – apparently exclusive, if not mutually antagonistic – theoretical schools, each with its own model of the discipline and its subject matter.

The picture becomes more complex again if we consider the many substantive specialisms, which can give every appearance of intellectual autonomy. There are sociologies of health and illness, religion and ritual, inequality and stratification, economic activity, kinship and the family, deviance, socialisation and education, culture, everyday life and interaction, organisations, politics, and gender relations, to mention only a few. Lastly, to muddy the waters even further, national sociologies – defined generically or otherwise – have their own intellectual histories and distinctive styles and concerns, the importance of which shouldn't be overlooked.

Sociologists are, in other words, a diverse crew. Some critics might go so far as to suggest that sociologists are indisciplined to the point of not being a discipline at all. I wouldn't agree. That sociology – even in its narrowest definition – is a broad church, short on articles of faith or consensus about its practices, seems to me to be a good rather than a bad thing, and it is certainly not my intention to suggest that this situation should change. Precisely because of the heterogeneity of its subject matter, the human world, sociology's greatest strength may well be its pluralism. And precisely because sociology is such a broad communion some minimal common ground seems to be vital. One of my objectives in this book is to offer some basic propositions about sociology's subject matter, and about its methods of investigation and analytical frameworks, which in principle – albeit very idealistic principle – might be acceptable across the widest possible range of the sociological spectrum. Hence the notion of sociological foundations.

The Roots of Sociology

As conventionally defined by the titles of university departments and degrees, sociology began as the study of the modern world. Auguste Comte first coined the word 'sociology' in 1838, to describe an emergent intellectual field that was seeking to understand better a world that, particularly in Europe and North America, was experiencing transformation at a rate and to an extent that appeared to be unprecedented. New ideas and vocabularies were needed for a dramatically new situation. That new situation was the coming-together of a number of closely connected developments, each of which continues to resonate globally at the beginning of the twenty-first century. These included:

- the runaway triumph of capitalism as the dominant way of organising production and distribution;
- the massive impact of industrialisation and mechanisation on humanity's productive powers and its capacities to transform the physical environment;
- the rationalisation of collective activities, most obviously the bureaucratisation of administration, production, law, and finance;
- the increasing number and size of cities;
- the flight from the land and the decay of long-established agrarian social systems and small-scale rural communities;
- the secularisation of the moral universe which attended organised religion's decline and the growing authority of rationalism and science;
- the proliferation of nominally democratic systems of government, particularly as constituted in concepts of individual citizenship rights and responsibilities;

- the emergence of new lines of social differentiation and conflict, in particular social class;
- the increasing size, prosperity and autonomy of the bourgeoisie, and the development of materialist individualism;
- the widespread migration, whether voluntary or forced, of unprecedented numbers of people, made possible by mechanised forms of transport, and bringing together in new locations peoples from an enormous diversity of origins; and
- the imposition of metropolitan, national cultures on peripheral populations, through the expansion of effective rule within their territories by nation-states, and the direct or indirect colonisation of all available spaces by global empires.

These developments, feeding off each other and given added force by their simultaneity, were seismic. They called sociology into existence, and provided it with the two intimately related tasks that have been its minimum unifying purpose ever since: to understand social change, and to fathom the relationship between the individual and the collective. Focusing on these is one of the most fruitful ways in which we can begin to specify sociology's subject matter.

It's obvious why it was important to get to grips with sweeping social change. Why the relationship between individuals and the collective was problematic is less self-evident. A number of factors were significant, and, of these, political change may have been decisive. Within the old established relationships of government – feudalism and absolutism – the object of individual political loyalties was obvious and concrete, if distant: the Emperor, the Queen, the Pope, the Elector, or whoever. Under the new constitutional regimes, however, it was increasingly more abstract – the State – and yet a good deal more intrusive. As subjects gradually became citizens, their consent, or at least their quiescence, had to be secured in new ways. Nor was this just a matter of concern for national governments. As organisations of different kinds became bigger and more impersonal, a similar question was posed for many collective enterprises.

Central to these developments in North America and much of Europe was the increasingly influential political creed that individuals, or at least certain kinds of individuals, possessed hitherto unimagined autonomy. As the other side of this coin, a politics of popular parties and organised movements also gradually appeared during the nineteenth century. In both respects the key question – well understood by Marx and Weber, for each of whom, albeit from contrasting positions, it provided the *leitmotif* for a life's work – was the nature of political action, the relationship between individual interests and collective organisation.

Other changes were significant, too. The seemingly irresistible tide of migration from country to town gave rise to widespread concerns that the local-level collective ties and reciprocal obligations of rural communities were being undermined and abandoned, with nothing developing in the cities to replace them. Ferdinand Tönnies first saw the problem; Durkheim and Simmel, from different directions, understood that it was at least as much opportunity as problem.[1] Durkheim and Weber realised that it was bound up with wider secularisation: the uncertain anxieties of individualism and a degree of moral autonomy were replacing the collective authority of religion.[2] Individualism was also connected to the rise of the bourgeoisie, not only as a significant political force but as a class of people with the leisure and surplus resources to devote to various life-style projects.

Nation-building, global migration and imperial expansion posed related questions. How could diverse peripheral and minority populations be brought within one national fold? With which collectivities – the local or the national – were people to identify? In this context Durkheim, for example, considered how a national education system could contribute to social integration.[3] In the United States the foundations of sociology were, in part, dug by the polyglot labouring masses that washed up on the shores of Ellis Island and the West Coast, bound for a future in which their children would become hyphenated Americans.[4] In America and throughout the European empires, a distinctive kind of sociology called anthropology began to emerge out of the forced incorporation of indigenous peoples into the cultural, political and economic systems of colonial powers.[5]

Wherever one looks during the nineteenth century, social change inspired questions about the nature of individuals and collectivities and the connections between them: questions about the relationships of citizens or subjects to the state, and about individualism and the decline of moral community. Even today, in a world which has since been transformed – although not out of all recognition, globalisation notwithstanding – understanding social change and the problematic relationship between the individual and the collective remain fundamental to sociology.

The Uses of Sociology

Examining the discipline's roots allows us to be clearer about sociology's usefulness. Sociology is not in any necessary sense about making the world a better place, or improving the lot of humankind. While there is nothing to prevent sociology contributing to either, both logic and whatever shaky lessons history can offer insist that a better understanding of that world and the human condition – leaving aside for the moment the question of what 'better' might mean in this context – may, in principle, be used for good or ill (supposing that the difference between the two is clear).

This is not necessarily the mainstream sociological view. Comte and many subsequent sociologists – naturally enough, given the intellectual climate of the times – expected sociology to become the 'science of society'. Some sociologists, of whom John Goldthorpe is an example, still aspire to this goal, albeit in moderate versions.[6] However, like many of the issues with which I am concerned in this book, the scientific status of sociology is not a purely intellectual issue. Throughout the nineteenth century and for most of the twentieth, progress and science were assumed to travel hand-in-hand. Marx, ever the optimist, certainly thought so. The only point of understanding the world was, after all, to change it, and for the better.[7] In this vein, sociology's contribution to improving the world has long been axiomatic, albeit vague, for most of its practitioners. At the beginning of the twenty-first century, however, even a mildly critical take on progress and the transformative power of knowledge encourages a humbled view of the possibilities. We don't have to embrace postmodern relativism to be sceptical about progress or to acknowledge the unintended dire consequences of science (any more than scepticism demands that we turn our backs on everything that has changed for the uncontroversial better).

Marx is a reminder that sociology and socialism share some historical roots. Socialism emerged from the same nineteenth-century turmoil and upheaval as sociology. Indeed, sociology is sometimes accused of being a species of socialism by another name. If sociology is what sociologists *do* – and have done – that accusation is, however, wide of the mark. Although eighteenth-century rationalism prepared a place for it, Comte first gave it a name, and Marx sketched out some of its most enduring ideas before his death in 1883, sociology as we know it today was established, institutionally and intellectually, by Weber, Simmel, Durkheim, and Mead. These names place sociology in historical context as a twentieth-century phenomenon and an indigenous inhabitant of the political centre ground. Radical enough in their sociological thinking – and frequently in their social comment – these men varied in their politics from the liberal to the social-conservative. None was a socialist.

The greatest relevance of Marx's work to sociology's founders, particularly Weber, may have been as a whetstone on which to hone many of their ideas. Their legacies, the great sociological traditions of functionalism, the action framework, and symbolic interactionism, overlap with Marx here and there, but Marxist sociology as such was largely a child of the 1950s and 1960s, a product of affluence and widening access to higher education. Serious political radicalism – which in recent sociology means feminism rather than Marxism, anyway – has historically been the sociological exception rather than the rule. It remains so today.

Towards a Generic Sociology

Acknowledging social change and the individual–collective relationship as the fundamental sociological themes has implications for the relationship between sociology and the other 'social studies', in particular social and cultural anthropology, social history, social psychology, social (or public) policy, and cultural studies. With respect to the first three, a strong case can be made for their inclusion under the broad umbrella of 'generic sociology' that I introduced at the end of the previous chapter. Each began as an intellectual response to the same upheavals and transformations which produced sociology, and, for each, understanding social change and the relationship between the collective and the individual are important. Their emphases may vary – social history prioritises social change and social psychology the individual end of the individual–collective relationship, while anthropology has eventually evolved a more even-handed set of concerns in all respects – but each is arguably a variation on the key sociological themes.

Social or public policy and cultural studies are more distant from sociology. Social policy is defined by a substantive topic agenda which reflects political concerns of one sort or another rather than underlying theoretical questions (which is not to suggest that it is a-theoretical or uninterested in, for example, social change). Social policy analysis is most accurately understood as a heterogeneous field of inquiry – *inter alia* it draws heavily on economics, political science and demography, as well as sociology – rather than a specialist branch of sociology. This doesn't prevent social policy analysis being sociological – it very often is – but it does mean that it isn't *necessarily* sociological.

Similar arguments apply to cultural studies. Here the intellectual agenda is framed by a notion of 'culture' which is largely unconcerned with the individual–collective relationship. With respect to theory and method, the distance between sociology and cultural studies is further underlined by the latter's historical roots in literary criticism and its contemporary dalliance with psychoanalysis. These influences can encourage an approach to theorisation which, while undoubtedly imaginative – and sometimes altogether inspiring – is too undisciplined by systematic empirical inquiry to fit into the model of sociology that I have in mind. Although many people working in cultural studies have strong intellectual affiliations with sociology, many others do not.

It is important to emphasise that the notion of generic sociology that I am proposing here isn't disciplinary imperialism by the back door. Sociology is too broadly-based and too internally prone to specialist balkanisation for that, and the other disciplines too well-developed and too institutionally secure to be vulnerable to a hostile take-over bid. All I am suggesting is that the intellectual similarities between sociology, social and cultural anthropology, social history, and social psychology are more convincing – and more creatively interesting – than their differences. If a symbolic umbrella is required under which to explore what we have in common, something called *generic sociology* is probably it. Furthermore, it seems to me that adopting this proposal potentially changes and widens the field of vision for all of these disciplines equally. What it does for sociology is to strip away the final vestiges of the notion that it is the specialist discipline which studies the industrialised modern world, liberating it to study the human world defined more generally.

It might be objected here, and not only by anthropologists, that a better umbrella would have 'anthropology' painted on it. As the generalist study of humanity this proposal has an obvious appeal: anthropology in this sense does indeed encompass all that the idea of 'generic sociology' might evoke. The problem is, however, that it encompasses many other things too. It is *too* broad: generic anthropology includes anthropological linguistics, physical anthropology – everything from bones to population genetics to the ethology of the great apes – and, some would still argue, archaeology. While, as is suggested by the arguments of Chapter Six, a better relationship to these disciplines would be an excellent idea, not least if it deepened sociology's sense of history, science is too fundamental to all of them for any closer relationship to be likely.

It might also be objected that in the notion of 'social science' or 'the social sciences' we already have a standard around which to muster the troops. This is also too broad. Drafting in everyone from human geographers to economists to political scientists to demographers, the social scientific high ground is crowded. These are all, what's more, subject areas which, much like social policy and cultural studies, define their boundaries and fields of vision according to fairly tightly defined substantive interests. United largely by defensive institutional considerations – not least competition with the humanities and the sciences – 'social science' has insufficient intellectual common purpose to foster authentic collective identification. A flag of convenience only, it doesn't prevent us from competing with each other for authority, credibility, status and money at least as ferociously as we do with everyone else. Taking into account sociology's contribution to liberal arts education in North America and elsewhere, and the fact that social history and anthropology have always had one foot in the humanities, it becomes increasingly clear that social science and generic sociology are not the same thing.

Finally – and unfortunately in the United Kingdom this argument has long been obscured by the attacks on 'social science' made by Tory politician Sir Keith Joseph during the 1980s – we ought to resist the confusion between sociology and science which the label of social science can encourage. Leaving aside questions about what scientists *actually* do in their everyday professional lives, it's clear enough that sociology can't do what science conventionally *claims* to do. The purpose of the scientific enterprise is not just to know, but to know in order to predict. To predict with at least some certainty, as a proper basis for rational intervention. This is why the experimental method and its analogues are so basic to science. The 'purest', most theoretical science is determinedly and definitively – even if only potentially – interventionist. This was true five hundred years ago for Leonardo da Vinci, when he wrote that, 'Science is the captain and practice the soldiers'[8], and it remains true today.

Of the 'social sciences', economics and psychology appear to be most comfortable with the business of prediction, even if we might wish to subject their claims in this respect – however hedged about with reservations – to the critical equivalent of a blow torch. Sociology, even in its most positivist, hard-nosed incarnations, really isn't comfortable with prediction any longer. Karl Marx and Herbert Spencer thought in terms of social laws, so in a weak sense did Emile Durkheim – even perhaps Max Weber – but we no longer do. Where we can, we get round this uncomfortable inability to achieve scientific rigour by talking about 'historical transitions' and the like, but we leave talk about laws to physicists and their ilk. As Margaret Archer has argued,[9] sociological guarantees are in their very essence dubious. When Anthony Giddens, for example, considers the future of a 'runaway world' he does so in balanced terms which are qualified by an appropriate awareness of the limited authority that can be brought to bear on the topic.[10]

The history of sociology has, in fact, been a passage from greater to lesser predictive certainty. We have progressively discovered what we should perhaps have known all along, that one of the defining features of the world of humans is its unpredictability and changeability. Humans are decision-making, reflexive creatures, given to bucking their own best-founded predictions. We are neither atoms nor amoeba. That we do something nine hundred and ninety-nine times in a row, doesn't mean that we will continue to do so (especially if someone – a sociologist, for example – points out to us that we're doing it). We look back and we talk back. We look forward, and we often don't do what we ourselves have predicted we will do. To bring Marx and Weber together, on the one hand we *shape* our lives under circumstances which are not of our own making; on the other, the meanings and histories of those lives routinely *take shape* out of the tragedy and farce of the unintended consequences of what we do.

Sociological epistemology and methodology – our varied concerns about how we are able to study the human world – are deeply implicated in this basic everyday uncertainty. Sociology is fundamentally not an experimental discipline. Research ethics aside, the organisational and other difficulties of putting together plausible experiments involving anything other than tiny numbers of people have long since decided that one. So, whether we participate in the action or not, we are by vocation observers of the human world rather than manipulators of it.

Where does this leave the argument for a robust everyday realism that I put forward in Chapter One? What of the necessary discipline that's imposed by having to attend to observable realities? Or the importance of empirically defensible generalisations about the human world and the immediate future? The discussion above suggests unambiguously the fundamental importance of epistemological modesty and of words such as 'plausibility' and 'defensibility'. It suggests that we should try to be clear about what we can and cannot be sure about, and under which circumstances. It suggests the claiming of an epistemological middle ground from which we can speak with some confidence to our contemporaries at large about the uncertainties of the human world. Perhaps even with some authority.

It also suggests that the word 'science' isn't really an appropriate partner for the word 'social', at least not as far as sociology is concerned. It may therefore be fortunate that my proposal to adopt the title of 'generic sociology' doesn't rest solely on rejecting the obvious alternatives. Intellectual history and genealogy are also on my side. Social anthropology owes its greatest theoretical debt to Durkheim, and more recently, via Clifford Geertz and Fredrik Barth, has been influenced by Weber, Erving Goffman and symbolic interactionism. Social history is utterly unthinkable without the inspiration of Weber and Marx, and its recent enthusiasm for the written and oral history of women, peasants, workers, and ordinary folk in general, is inspired in part by the ethnographic traditions of anthropology and sociology. Similarly, the influence on social psychology of G. H. Mead, symbolic interactionism and Goffman should not be underestimated (although it can be overstated too). Sociology itself has always provided sanctuary for renegade anthropologists, historians and social psychologists, and has always profited intellectually thereby.

Perhaps the greatest weakness of my argument is the assumption that a generic umbrella is a good idea: that talking to each other, recognising our intellectual similarities as well as our differences, is viable and desirable. As a well-intentioned and unapologetic liberal, I believe that talking to each other is always better than not: 'being as reasonable as we are able to be, we ought all to argue'.[11] I am also, however, saying something a little more specific. In the first place, as I have just suggested, a common intellectual heritage and purpose already exists. Although they need some attention and maintenance – hence the arguments of this book – we don't have to conjure them out of thin air. All I am proposing is that we recognise that we are engaged in the same business, concerned with the same questions, and that we share more, intellectually, than not.

There may also be a potential that isn't being achieved. In this respect all we have is a choice, which we are free, individually and collectively, to refuse: to remain where we are, or to explore the more-than-the-sum-of-the-parts that a generic sociology might turn out to be. To see where that journey might take us. It might be nowhere, or nowhere special, but in the absence of trying it we'll never know whether this might be the road out of the bureaucratised rut of intellectual routine into which much sociology has quietly slumped. The extravagant promises of postmodernism and its fellow travellers seem to have led nowhere, at best, and into the swamp, at worst. It may be time to try something else, and a co-operative attempt to revitalise the common heritage on which our collective efforts rest might be a good place to start.

Sociological Sense and Common Sense

If generic sociology is ever to be something more than a catch-phrase – and if we are ever to forge the better relationship to the people we study that our subject demands – we need a working consensus about how the understandings and explanations of the human world offered by generic sociology differ from everyday understandings and explanations. If any kind of sociology is to be worth having, it must offer something other than common sense, and it must be able to justify what it offers as valuable, if not actually preferable. Moreover, if we are to communicate successfully with a wider audience than ourselves, our arguments for sociology cannot depend on either rubbishing common sense, or claiming a qualitatively special kind of wisdom (as, arguably, do the takes on this issue offered by Alfred Schutz or Pierre Bourdieu, for example[12]). The first would defeat the point – if common sense were rubbish, there'd be little need to justify sociological sense – while the second challenges the possibility of any dialogue between common sense and sociological sense.

So, in what ways *does* sociological sense differ from common sense? Is it simply in our concerns with social change and the relationships between individuals and collectivities? These were central to the defence of sociology provided by C. Wright Mills, when he defined the most fruitful work of the sociological imagination as the bringing together of public issues and private troubles – history and biography – and the understanding of each in the context of the other.[13] I wish I'd thought of something half as elegant, or half as resonant.

Unfortunately, if this was an adequate manifesto for sociology in 1959 – and with the benefit of hindsight I don't think it was – it certainly isn't adequate now. It seems to offer a vision of sociology as a discipline largely, or even solely, concerned with social problems. Not only is this a surrender to utilitarianism – albeit in Mills's case, despite his strictures on practicality and his traditionalist closing precepts on intellectual craftsmanship,[14] a relatively radical utilitarianism – but it overlooks the straightforward truth that not every sociologically interesting aspect of the human world is either an issue or a problem. Furthermore, since public issues and private troubles, history and biography – social change and its consequences for individual lives – are a staple of everyday conversation and common sense, nor can this definition help us to understand better the relationship between common sense and sociological sense.

The separate arguments of Peter Berger and Zygmunt Bauman,[15] that sociology is the art of seeing the general in the particular, fall at the same fence. They don't differentiate sociology sufficiently clearly from common sense. Just listen to everyday talk as it goes on around you and as you participate in it. We don't need to put on our sociological hats to situate our particular individual experiences within more general historical and interpretive frameworks. We do it all the time: as humans, it is probably more difficult to avoid than it is to do.

Perhaps what really matters, then, is *how* we talk about our basic sociological themes. According to Bauman, 'thinking sociologically' is different from, and preferable to, common sense in the following ways:[16]

- sociology is an example of 'responsible speech', dependent for its authority on rational, organised, and logically structured arguments, and on appeals to evidence that are open to public scrutiny;
- sociology, in its ability to marshal a wide range of information and argument, should command a broader field of vision on the social world than common sense; and
- sociology makes distinctive sense of the human world from a perspective which begins with the collective, understanding individuals within 'webs of interdependency'.

If Bauman is saying that common sense is individualistic, while sociology makes its sense in collective terms, he is wrong (or, at least, he is much too definite). Common sense includes a routine and well-developed sense of collective interdependency: we, us, them, family, community, fellowship, nation, and so on, feature routinely in everyday conversation. Coming from the other direction, sociology is, by definition, concerned with persons (the individual–collective relationship is, after all, at its core) and some versions of sociology are resolutely focused, theoretically and in their research methods, on the individual.

As an anthropology graduate student doing fieldwork, I wrestled with the differences between my understandings of life on a housing estate in north Belfast and the understandings of the people who lived there, some of whom were interested in, and sceptical of, my attempts to make a sense of their lives which wasn't the sense that they made. They believed, for example, that unemployed people, particularly unemployed young people, simply didn't want to work. That was why they were unemployed. I thought the matter was less simple, a combination of what the young people themselves did or didn't do and a complex of other factors, many of which were to be found outside the everyday life of the locality.[17] I came up with a three-fold justification of sociological sense that isn't quite the same as Bauman's. Two decades later I have refined it slightly but I still can't come up with anything better:[18]

- as a result of *systematic inquiry*, sociologists should have access to more, and more detailed, information than is routinely available in everyday life;
- sociology should strive towards *objectivity*, pursuing its own ends rather than those of participants, and correspondingly be able to pay attention to all the points of view represented in any situation; and
- sociology's own ends are generalisation, analysis, and communication, in a word the *theory* which liberates sociology from the concrete specificities of local common sense, and opens up wider possibilities of critique and revision.

Responsible speech and the size of the field. Systematic inquiry, objectivity, and theory. Taken together – and allowing for their differences with respect to the collective – these propositions amount to a plausible argument that, although common sense and sociological sense inhabit the same world, and although sociology cannot claim a dramatically different *kind* of knowledge, the two are not the same, and sociology can defend its claim to be able to make better sense of the human world.

Bauman argues, further, that sociology's special assignment is to 'defamiliarise the familiar'.[19] Now this isn't a unique mission – after all, what else does much art do? – but we might expect no less of sociology, as an intellectual offspring of modernity, and a grandchild of the Enlightenment. Nor is it a dramatically new suggestion. Some of the micro-sociologies which came out of the United States in the 1950s attempted to render everyday, taken-for-granted social reality 'anthropologically strange', in order to reap the analytical harvest offered by the vision of one's own culture as exotically unfamiliar. The result was a series of studies whose needlepoint detail was only matched by their tunnel-vision and, arguably, their banality.[20] This suggests that rendering the familiar unfamiliar, whether it be seeing the universe in a grain of sand or prising the scales from one's eyes, may not be easy. But if it's a worthwhile goal – and it is, if only because of the subversive possibilities that it opens up – then sociology seems to me to be well-placed to attempt it. Systematic inquiry, objectivity, and theory all aim in that direction.

The Necessity of Theory

To concentrate for the moment on theory, it seems to be one of the most misunderstood aspects of sociology, by both its defenders and its critics. Theory certainly shouldn't be an end in itself. That it seems to have become so renders the question, 'What's the *point* of theory?' – which is among the most common questions asked by non-sociologists and students – easy to understand and even easier to sympathise with. If we are to answer it satisfactorily, and if we are ever to remedy the estrangement between general social theory and the observable realities documented by empirical research, we need to begin with what theory is, and what it isn't. Defined as broadly as possible, sociological theorising involves the creation of abstract models of those observable realities, in order to aid our better understanding of what goes on in the world of humans. Sociological theory is the distinctive interpretive framework within and through which we make sociological sense of the human world. Particularly in generalisation and analysis, theory is at the core of sociology's distinctive perspective on the human world.

Generalisation – focusing on the wider context as a matter of sociological principle – depends on abstraction. This means that, for sociology, there isn't a 'no theory' option. Generalisation involves classifying together aspects of the human world and using the categories generated to make sense of that world. Sociological categorisation, like any other, involves establishing comparative relationships of similarity and difference between observable phenomena, and locating and identifying phenomena as specific instances of general categories. Sociological general categories are, however, what Weber called 'ideal types',[21] which don't necessarily correspond to the facts of any particular observable reality. That any member of a sociological category is unlikely to conform to all of the ideal criteria which define that category exemplifies the necessary imprecision which investigating the human world demands: humans and their works are too variable and changeable for anything else. If our categories are not to be subject to perpetual fission – to the absurd point where each would decline to a membership of one – or too unstable over time to be usable, there is no other choice than the 'fuzzy categorisation' of ideal types. Without them sociology would be impossible.

Generalisation also requires us to be clear about what are appropriate objects of our sociological attention, and what kinds of connections they can have with each other. It would be impossible to establish useful conceptual categories if we didn't have some sense of their basic building blocks. In other words, generalisation requires that we have a view on the ontology of the human world. As the philosophical discourse about the metaphysics of being, ontology is concerned with what can be said to exist in the universe: the ontology of the human world is concerned with what can be said to exist in the human world. From my point of view its fundamental question is, 'What are the phenomena with which sociology is concerned?'

In this most basic sense, the business of sociology is with human individuals, their recurrent practices and products, and human collectivities. How we can best understand these will be discussed further in Chapters Three and Four. The specification of *which* individuals, patterns of behaviour, and collectivities matter depends on our focus in any specific empirical context, and is the business of substantive theory.

The ontology of the world of humans necessarily rests on another ontology, i.e. how we understand whatever counts as 'everything else'. Sociology may not be science, but it is a rationalist enterprise, and with respect to the wider context of which the world of humans is a part, we assume that we inhabit an approximately Newtonian physical universe. The connections that we believe we can establish between our conceptual building blocks are conditioned by this assumption.

To illustrate how this matters, let's consider the early modern witch hunts in Europe and the American colonies.[22] Any sociological analysis of these events will, almost certainly, be founded on axiomatic assumptions that the women accused of witchcraft couldn't fly, and that magic or bewitchment didn't work in the way they were believed to work. How we understand the basic analytical categories of 'witches' and 'witchcraft' thus depends upon our ontology of the 'natural world'. That *any* sociological category does is an argument to which I will return in Chapter Six.

Central to generalisation is *comparison*: between different categories and their members in the same context, or between similar categories across space or time. Without the context-independent comparison offered by generalisation and abstraction, sociology as we know it wouldn't be possible. The wider truth here is that generalisation and abstraction are fundamental to language, and without them the human world would lack either a past or a future. Language allows us to evoke things that are not present and manipulate them intellectually in complex ways. It is central to the human imagination. Without generalisation and abstraction, human consciousness would be trapped in a specific here-and-now, and our understanding of the human world would, at best, be non-cumulative. How complex our understanding of anything could be is debatable. There wouldn't even be a world of humans as we experience it: collect-ivities, which are fine examples of the human capacity for generalisation and abstraction, would simply not be meaningful.

Talking about comparison moves the discussion on to *analysis*, the second component of theory. Analysis requires that we spe-cify our problem or question, and what kinds of solutions or answers – explanations or interpretations, for example – are acceptable. Problems or questions, and solutions or answers, are closely intertwined moments in the evolution of our under-standing (as are generalisation and abstraction). In formulating problems and questions we are identifying what it is that we want to understand better, which presupposes some prior under-standing of what the appropriate objects of sociological analysis are. Nor can one identify phenomena, or attempt to account for them, without having a view about the connections that can possibly exist between them. The establishment of plausible connections, and their exploration, is the basic business of analysis.

By way of an example, returning to the witchcraft persecu-tions, our assumption that witches couldn't fly or really bewitch people has implications for how we analyse the problem socio-logically. Those people accused of the Satanic Pact, of flying off to kiss the Devil's arse on a mountain top, or of putting a blight on their neighbour's milk, were, by our definition, innocent. We simply do not accept that they *could* have done most of the things of which they were accused. The accusation and execution of so many people appears in one light if we think they were innocent as charged, in quite another if they were guilty. Simi-larly, positing the existence of an underground pagan religion of whom 'witches' were members – membership of which we can at least accept as a Newtonian possibility – is very different from focusing on the fact that the majority of the accused were women, and invoking misogyny as the motor of this par-ticular history.[23] Some people don't believe in the existence of secret religions; others deny the ubiquity of misogyny. Different ontologies – different versions of what we're interested in, and thus of what's defined as possible – in different degrees of abstraction, generate different problems and questions, which necessarily mean different solutions and answers (although they *may* be offered side-by-side, in the intellectual promiscuity that often characterises the best analyses). These are theoretical matters, and are unavoidable if we are to analyse the matter at all.

The fastidiousness with which I have chosen my words so far indicates the presence of a problem. I have talked about 'analysis', 'solutions' and 'answers' in order to avoid choosing between 'interpretation' and 'explanation'.[24] This distinction, first formulated in nineteenth-century Germany, remains important to many philosophers and methodologists: scientific *explanation* is believed to involve identifying objective causal relationships between phenomena in the human world, while humanistic *interpretation* prioritises the meanings and motivations of humans. Each appears to invoke contrasting ontologies of the human world. The distinction is also a clash of epistemologies, of ways to know the world and to justify the claim to knowledge.

However, the more one examines it, the less clear the distinction between explanation and interpretation becomes. Sociology involves making sense of the behavioural patterns we observe in the world of humans. Making sense means asking either *how* something comes about, or *why*. Each involves choosing among an array of possible connections that can exist between the phenomena in question. However, each question can involve looking for causes or interpretations, and each can be answered with reference to either 'objective' causes or 'subjective' motivation and meaning. In the sociological appreciation of the unintended consequences of action – something for which we have Weber to thank[25] – explanation and interpretation collide: the human world turns on both patterns of cause and effect *and* reflexive meanings and decision-making.

Furthermore, the process of making sociological sense of what humans do in terms of its causes doesn't differ dramatically from making interpretive sense. This is what I take Goldthorpe,

for example, to mean, when he insists that there is only one
sociological logic of inference:[26] formulating sociological categories by generalisation and abstraction from specific instances,
inferring the connections that are likely to exist between them
to produce the observable reality in question, and regularly
keeping an eye on how our conclusions measure up to our data
about that observable reality. Ethnographers do this no less than
statisticians, and general theorists often don't do it all. There is
no inevitable sequence in which to do it, and the rigour with
which we do it is vulnerable to pragmatism, institutional pressures, and the smugness of conventional wisdom, but, in ideal-
typical terms, this is what we do. In sociological research of
whatever kind, analysis – specifying the connections between
phenomena – *always* involves some sense of causality and some
attention to actors' meanings. We need both, to make sense of
the world of humans.

Theory's third characteristic is – or at least *should* be – a concern
with *communication*, the manner in which generalisation and
analysis are combined in an abstract version of some aspect of the
human world, which attempts to make sense of the observable
realities of which it is an abstraction. Different kinds of generalisation and analysis are likely to have different communicative
implications, and we have at our disposal three basic media for
presenting them: *words*, *numbers*, and what for want of a better
word I will call *pictures* (everything from actual pictures to graphs
and charts).

Here we are concerned with clarity of presentation rather
than obscurity, and with the question of the audience that sociology should be addressing, matters to which I will return in
the closing chapter. That isn't all, however. The communicative
dimension of theory is particularly important because with it,
ideally, comes an explicit concern with our models. Model-
building is about connecting general categories to produce
analytical accounts which help us to understand better the
human world, accounts which are more-than-the-sum-of-their-
constituent-parts. Which are, in other words, sociological. Our
communicative strategies are thus integral to our theories. They

are not a residual matter, something to which we attend once the important business is out of the way. The medium is definitely part of the message.

So, sociological theory combines three elements. The first is the specification of the general categories that encompass the phenomena which make up the observable reality of the human world, and of the kinds of connections that we think are possible between them. The second, analysis, involves formulating problems or questions, and offering solutions or answers in the shape of identifying plausible connections between the phenomena in which we are interested. Thirdly, these must be brought together into an acceptable model of the situation which allows the whole to be communicated. These are not necessarily consecutive stages, even though that is how they are often presented in text books: theorisation is a more messy process than is often allowed for.

To return to the relationship between common sense and sociological sense, it might be argued that sociologists have no monopoly on generalisation, analysis, or communication. That's true: the models which people put together in their everyday conversations in order to make sense of their lives and the world around them, exhibit all of these characteristics. What is typically absent from everyday common sense, however, is the *explicit* and *reflexive* combination of generalisation, analysis and communication in an attempt to elucidate and understand regular patterns of human behaviour. In the process – especially when systematic inquiry and objectivity are brought into the frame – something more than the sum-of-the-common-sensical-parts emerges. Sociological theory necessarily bears a family resemblance to everyday theory, but it isn't the same thing.

The discussion so far has only implicitly addressed the problematic relationship between theory and research. Although theorists often comfort themselves by reflecting that empirical research is impossible without theory – and this is absolutely true – they typically neglect to recognise that for sociologists this is no less true the other way round. Our general concepts don't just appear, like Venus from the conch shell, they have to be abstracted *from something*, and that something can only be the observable realities of the human world. There is nothing else. What's more, if we want our general concepts to transcend common sense *and* avoid metaphysics, it's necessary that our knowledge of this 'something' should be systematically constructed, based in research rather than haphazard hearsay or observation.

Objectivity as defined in the previous chapter – the attempt to stand back from the human world in order to see as much as possible of what's going on, as clearly as possible – also demands general concepts based in systematic inquiry. The distance created by objectivity necessarily entails a degree of abstraction. What is more, objectivity requires that our basic categories should be as free from bias as we can make them. It may be an imperfect defence, but only systematic inquiry offers the kind of access to observable reality which can hope to keep ideology at bay. And only systematic inquiry offers sufficient transparency of method to encourage the criticism and inspection of our evidence about the world of humans that is vital, if aiming for the most objective view possible is to be something other than a pious hope.

The most objective possible views of the human world should also, in principle, be the best views possible. This doesn't, however, mean that they will necessarily converge or concur. That much is guaranteed by sociology's intellectual pluralism. None the less there is some firm, and relatively consensual, ground available to us. That sociology is the study of regular and recurrent patterns in the human world is uncontroversial. So too – probably – are the connected themes of social change and the relationship between the individual and the collective. My argument for the interconnection and indispensability of theory *and* systematic inquiry may command less support, however. The ontology of the human world, the basic nature of our subject matter, ought to be a matter for agreement, but it probably isn't either, not least because it's largely taken for granted. This is the subject of the next chapter.

Three
Society and Culture

Talking about 'the human world' or 'the world of humans' is a conscious attempt on my part to avoid established terminology, in the cause of shedding fresh light on the conceptual foundations of sociology. Before going any further, however, I want to consider more closely the words which sociologists conventionally use to talk about the human world, particularly the closely connected notions of 'society' and 'culture'. Two of the most important words in sociology, these refer in a very general fashion, in different contexts and with different emphases, to the whatever-it-is-that-is-more-than-the-sum-of-the-parts that sociologists take to be their subject matter.

These notions are central to the typically taken-for-granted ontology of the human world on which a great deal – perhaps all – of sociology rests. They are so fundamental that if we want to be clear about sociology's possibilities and limitations we must first be clear about 'society' and 'culture'. What's more, this is a timely issue given that these notions, caught in the intellectual backwash of postmodernism and the widening net of globalisation, are increasingly seen as deeply problematic by some social theorists. John Urry, for example, marked the sociological millennium by remarking that, although the discipline is premised upon the concept of 'society', what that concept actually means is unclear.[1] Similarly, Terry Lovell, characterising culture as a 'ravening concept', suggests that our proclivity for understanding everything as 'cultural' has deprived the concept of its analytical value.[2]

It's also important to be clear about 'society and culture' because as words which occur frequently in everyday conversation they offer a further opportunity to look at the relationship

between sociology and common sense. Whereas in Chapter Two
I focused on the differences between common sense and sociology, looking at 'society' and 'culture' allows us to see something of what they share, where they overlap and in which
respects.

Society

What are the common-sense meanings of 'society'? A quick
trawl through a couple of good dictionaries quickly produces a
number of clear-cut options. First, and least abstract, we find
collectivities such as The Ulster Society for the Prevention of
Cruelty to Animals, The Society of Friends, The Royal Society
of Arts, The John Birch Society, The Anti-Slavery Society,
The Society of Jesus, The Audubon Society, The Society for
Promoting Christian Knowledge, or La Société Nationale des
Chemins de Fer Française. A society in this sense is a formal
organisation, set up to achieve specified ends. The conduct of
its affairs is at least notionally governed by rules and regulations,
it has an internal structure of offices and functions, it is legally
and economically constituted as a corporate body, and it has a
definite membership, recruited according to specific criteria and
procedures. A 'society' in this sense serves as the framework
within which its members pursue the goals for which it was
established, and may represent the interests of, and act on behalf
of, its members, collectively and sometimes individually: individual and collective interests are identified with each other to
some extent.

Secondly, there is an old-fashioned usage – it would have
made perfect sense to either Jane Austen or F. Scott Fitzgerald –
which, if the popularity of movies such as *Four Weddings and a
Funeral* is any indication, remains current and is fascinating to
many people. It is still possible to talk meaningfully about 'polite
society', 'a society wedding', perhaps even 'being presented
to society'. This 'society' is a very definite collective arena,
constituted less by explicit regulation than by notions of background and breeding, by etiquette, manners, and use of language,

and by money, although the distinction between old and new money is crucial.[3] It is an extended network for organising and facilitating the reproduction of the élite, culturally and in the more down-to-earth sense of bloodlines and new blood.[4] While the calendar of this society is constructed around formally organised events such as balls, parties, weddings, certain horse racing meetings,[5] polo matches, and regattas, and membership is a function of belonging to formal organisations, particularly exclusive clubs, schools and the officer corps, the crucial thing is allegiance to, and participation in, an accepted and appropriate way of doing things. To its members this is probably the only world that matters. To a greater or lesser degree, one suspects, all else is irrelevant: how else to make sense of this charmless – even if innocently unselfconscious – appropriation of the notion of 'society'?

A less élitist, but none the less related, use of the word 'society' simply refers to the company of other humans. A recluse, for example, can be said to be 'avoiding society'. Here the word invokes some sense of a public collective space, and of sociability, if not necessarily conviviality. Here 'society' simply means collectivity and people in relationships with each other. Related usages might include descriptions of humans as 'social animals', or a particular individual as 'sociable'.

The next meaning of the word, in which 'society' is the general collectivity to which we belong – however that 'we' is defined, and from whatever point of view – is obviously closely related. From 'our' point of view a convict, for example, having repaid his debt to society (or even *her* debt, although that's statistically much less likely), can be said to rejoin society on release from prison. However, from the internal point of view of its inmates – whether prisoners or guards – the prison can itself reasonably be understood as a society in microcosm.[6] This sense of 'society' is always defined from a specific point of view and is predicated on exclusion as well as inclusion: being 'in' means that someone is 'out'; an 'us' always implies a 'them'.

It is in this sense that newspapers and politicians regularly and enthusiastically conjure up images of 'society'. We are all familiar with expressions such as 'society today', 'making a better society', 'a threat to society', or the 'kind of society that we want our children to grow up in'.[7] In reverse, there is the argument, which in Britain will probably forever be associated with Margaret Thatcher,[8] that 'there is no such thing as society'. What's being evoked in this meaning of the word is a sense of collective life in general and its nature; a sense of <u>membership</u> and belonging; a sense of <u>mutual expectations</u>, obligations and norms; a sense of established patterns of doing things and institutions; a sense of something wider and more abstract than the interests and business of the immediate here and now. A sense that there *is* such a thing as society.

A well-established variation on this theme – which actively deploys the 'them' as well as the 'us' – appears when we talk about different 'societies'. We might talk about England or France or the United States as different societies. In this sense, Canadian 'society' is not the same as American 'society', and Mexico is a different 'society' again. This usage is heavily imbued with the <u>historical legacy of the nation-state</u>.[9] In the context of an international system of relationships between distinct nation-states, the state has in fact become mapped onto the notion of 'society'. However, this correspondence between the state and 'society' is neither ubiquitous nor precise: it's perfectly reasonable to say, for example, that Québécois 'society' differs from Anglo-Canadian 'society'. Viewed from a greater distance, whether as archaeologists or educational-television-watching members of the public, we are comfortable talking about entities such as Ancient Egyptian 'society' or Mayan 'society'. In all of these related usages, 'society' calls up an image of characteristic collective ways of doing things and bounded patterns of collective organisation and belonging.

Lastly, and closely related to the previous two, there is perhaps the most abstract sense of human collectivity, summed up in expressions such as 'hunter-gatherer society', 'the consumer society', 'medieval society', 'Western society', or 'the information society'. While the emphasis, once again, is on characteristic ways of doing things, characteristic styles of life, and characteristic shared experiences, the perspective here is the most general possible, in that it doesn't depend on the evocation of fixed boundaries. Nor is it completely abstract. Even its ultimate expression – 'human society' – may one day be a more substantial reality than it is in contemporary rhetoric about the international or global community.

Looking at these common-sensical meanings of 'society' side by side, as I have just done, suggests that they have three features in common:

- first, each refers to networks of people relating to each other in some meaningful way, even if only indirectly;
- second, there are criteria of membership, and therefore there is some sense of inclusive – and therefore necessarily exclusive – boundedness; and
- third, each conveys a sense of ways of doing things in common, of characteristic patterns of behaviour, of organisation.

These meanings of 'society' also suggest that there is widespread recognition that there is something more to everyday life than the embodied obviousness of individuals. However, it isn't possible to see, touch, hear, taste, or smell 'society', in the way that it is possible to see, touch, hear, taste, and smell individuals. This explains, in part, why the assertion that 'there's no such thing as society' makes a kind of sense. The observable reality is that 'society' simply doesn't exist in the same way that individuals do.

Which leaves us in something of a quandary, caught between the definiteness of our sense of collectivity and its elusive substance. One route out of this cul-de-sac is to ask why we humans talk about 'society', or something similar, at all. I want to propose that we do so because the notion addresses a number of pressing, and related, existential issues with which we are routinely confronted.

The first of these is rooted in the mundane practicalities of how humans think and manage information.[10] The sensory here-and-now of immediate experience does not begin to constitute even a tiny part of the human world as we routinely experience it. That world is simply too extensive and too complex, even in small-scale collectivities and settings, to be taken in at one go. The smallest spatial arena contains so much information of interest to humans that in order to manage it cognitively – to boil it down to intellectually manageable proportions – we need to be able to generalise and to abstract. We simply cannot deal with or communicate our experience of the everyday human world solely in the immediately concrete terms of the individuals who we see, with whom we interact, and to whom we relate. Talking only about concrete individuals would render it impossible to include everything we need to know about or understand for competent functioning in the human world. As a closely related point, we also need to be able to think about and refer to other humans in the abstract, when they aren't present, and even perhaps without ever having met them. This means having available to us general categories of types of human, which necessarily implies a degree of collectivity, or at least some thinking in collective terms.

Secondly, as Durkheim, for example, recognised in *The Elementary Forms of the Religious Life*,[11] there are many everyday human phenomena which from the point of view of participants are often not experientially reducible to individual behaviour. Obvious examples of this include the 'we-ness' of family, lineage and ethnicity, the shared emotion aroused by effective ritual occasions (whether sacred or profane), tasks and occasions involving the successful co-ordination of activity and effort by two or more people (think of a sports team in action), and the complexities of impersonal crowd behaviour in public. In all of these, something other than the purely individual seems, to us as participants, to be occurring, something that is 'more-than-the-sum-of-the-parts'.

Thirdly, and in the longer term, many of those phenomena that we recognise as collectivities obviously persist over time, even though their individual members or constituents come and go, and even though they – whatever 'they' might be –

persistently and routinely change in their rules, regulations, functions, and so on.[12] There is an enduring imagination of reality to be found in our sense of collectivity. Change and the continuity of collectivities do not preclude each other: they go together, hence the close connection between the study of social change and the relationship between the individual and the collective.

Finally, and more speculatively, if there is something that we can call human nature – and in Chapter Six I will argue that there is – then part of that nature may simply be the capacity, and perhaps the need, to go beyond the visible, to imagine something other than 'what there is': in this case something that is 'us' and is also, at the same time, 'more than us'. Certainly this is something that humans seem always to have done: beliefs about the supernatural, the laws of physics, and notions of 'society' are, in this limited sense, equivalents. All involve going beyond the immediate evidence of our senses (and all are attempts to make sense of that evidence). At least in part, this is what John Donne was pointing to when he insisted that none of us is an island, entire unto ourselves.[13] Humans do not exist in isolation: we are collective animals. Why else is solitary confinement such an effective and cruel punishment to impose on a human being? So, of course, we need to talk about the collective aspects of our lives, if only because, in a very real sense, every aspect of our lives as individuals is tied in to collectivity. Solipsism is not the human condition.

Each of these issues, not least the last, is something which we can all experience and recognise in our everyday lives. They are neither metaphysical nor exotic. They are, in fact, very mundane. Woven together they add another strand to our understanding of why the relationship between the individual and the collective should be so definitive of sociology.

So, what do sociologists mean when they talk about 'society' (or equivalent expressions such as 'the social world')? First, we mean the same abstract, more-than-the-sum-of-parts reality that is meant by the word in everyday common sense, denoting membership, a sense of collectivity, and organised ways of

doing things. However, we talk about this in sociologically
characteristic ways, including the following:

- as the network of actually-existing relationships between
  individuals;
- as regularity and pattern in human behaviour;
- as institutional structure and inter-relatedness;
- as a system of interacting 'social forces';
- as some kind of abstract collective agent which acts on or
  influences individuals;
- as the embodiment of shared norms and values; and
- as historical periods, epochs, and eras.

There are several things which it is important to understand
about these sociological versions of 'society'. In sociological
speech, for example, they are typically used every bit as impre-
cisely and vaguely as they are in everyday common sense.
However, in reflection of the fact that the human world is at
least in part ordered, and of the need, if we are to make any
sociological sense of it, to categorise information and data and
organise them into abstract and general models, the sociological
understanding of 'society' is heavily imbued with notions of
system, structure, inter-relatedness, and organisation.

In part as a result of this – although it isn't inevitable – there
is a tendency to imagine 'society' as more concrete than it is, to
talk about it as a 'thing', different from, and in opposition to,
individuals. Sociological notions of system and structure have
been influential in creating an image of 'society' as somehow in
opposition to, or over and against, individuals. This is a version
of our central sociological theme of the relationship between
the individual and the collective that has been immortalised in
generations of undergraduate essays dealing with the structure –
action debate, the relationship between the micro and the
macro, and, most recently, structuration theory.

Allowing for the above, this reification of 'society' is also, in
part, a reflection of the undoubted difficulties involved in successfully capturing the elusive more-than-the-sum-of-the-parts

of the human world, in recognising that while 'society' is imagined – in that it is a creation of humans – it is not imaginary. That society isn't a 'thing' cannot be taken to mean that 'there's no such thing as society'.

The Social, the Cultural, the Economic

Something called 'the individual' isn't the only thing to which the notion of 'society' is often opposed. 'Society' is also frequently contrasted with 'culture', the other common concept to which we resort in our attempt to imagine successfully the more-than-the-sum-of-the-parts. One familiar version of this dualism is to talk about the cultural as mental or intellectual, encompassing knowledge, ideas, values, attitudes, and so on. The social in this light may be seen as more concrete, perhaps even more real: it's what people do, visible interaction and behaviour, actual institutions.

This way of understanding the human world often also distinguishes 'the economic' as a further separate domain of material needs and their satisfaction and self-interested rationality.[14] In addition, long-established utilitarian and materialist habits of thought may privilege the economy as more substantial and real than society. Thus we have an ontological continuum, from the material to the ideal. From the more real to the less real. From the more important to the less important, the significant to the trivial. From the economic, to the social, to the cultural. From the concrete individual – the basic particle of economics – to the collective abstraction of culture.

Crude materialism is often identified with Marxism, but it is probably even more deeply ingrained in liberal free-market economics. It is also characteristic of much everyday common sense in the industrialised world. This view of the world is, however, historically and locally specific. Many theologies, for example, understand the material world of appearances as an illusion. The cosmologies of many peoples around the globe recognise the existence of more things in heaven and earth than materialist ontology can possibly dream of. As an ideology of the financial bottom line, of the subjugation and exploitation of the natural world, it owes its genesis and subsequent intellectual pre-eminence to the power of capitalism and universal abstract money, on the one hand, and the Enlightenment separation of the mental from the physical, mind from body, on the other.[15]

Securely established as a pervasive set of organising principles throughout institutionalised education in the industrialised world, this model of the world finds one expression in the current low political status of the arts and humanities, and the high status of the sciences: residual cultural cachet is one thing, power and influence another.[16] It has also created the social sciences, that loose confederation of activities discussed in Chapter Two which strive perpetually to position themselves at the right end of this status hierarchy. Within the social sciences, it is the rationale for competitive departments of economics, psychology, sociology and cultural studies. In the case of psychology, it eggs on a dominant perspective which, in the name of a precious − if precarious − claim to science, attempts to reduce the mental to the physically and mechanically measurable. Ultimately, it generates a model of the human world that is created in the image of the organisation of university departments and faculties.[17]

This creaky division of intellectual labour can be exemplified by looking briefly at the different frameworks which have been used to understand one of the more striking aspects of the organisation of industrialised, capitalist human collectivities. The observable reality in this particular respect is that industrial capitalism is characterised by significant differences, in their access to resources of all kinds, between the élite and the rest of the population. The latter have to rely on the sale of their labour power in order to achieve significant access to resources at all. These differences can be so extreme that those at the bottom may lack sufficient food, shelter and clothing, while those at the top engage in extensive displays of conspicuous consumption.

Surveying the literature,[18] this hierarchical organisation of human life under capitalism can be thought about culturally, socially, and economically, as in the schema below.

Cultural

- Stratification as produced and reproduced by cultures of poverty.
- Class as culture, as a distinctive way of life.
- Social stratification as a status hierarchy of occupations and skills.
- Social class as competitive position with respect to various markets, such as employment, housing and education.

Social

- Stratification as a hierarchical continuum of occupation, differential access to resources, and networks of interaction.
- Class as the relationship to the means of production.
- Stratification as the pattern of differential rewards accruing to rational individual decision-making in education and the labour market.
- Stratification as differential rewards for differential individual endowments and productivity.
- Stratification as a descriptive model of quantifiable individual differences of wealth (possessions and/or income).

Economic

This is a necessarily crude – and *very* incomplete – typification of an enormous body of broadly sociological writing, published over many decades. It arguably leaves out more than it includes, it draws sharp distinctions between traditions of research which in reality may be more difficult to tease out from each other, and it ignores the fact that it's possible to subscribe to some of these positions simultaneously. It also neglects recent research and debates which draw upon wider and more multi-dimensional notions of inclusion and exclusion.[19]

This list is, however, only intended to make one basic point: that the concepts listed are different ways of talking about what is essentially one phenomenon: the inequality which characterises capitalism. And it is striking just *how* different these points of view are. Fundamental ontological assumptions, which take for granted as 'real' a hierarchy of distinctions between the economic, the social, and the cultural domains – or which distinguish between the reality and significance of individuals and collectivities – are enormously influential in steering how we attend to and understand the human world.

To return to the distinction between the social and the cultural, I have suggested that it's often understood in terms of a blunt contrast between thinking and doing, between 'cultural' meaning and 'social' behaviour. This contrast begs some obvious and important questions. To begin with, thinking is an activity, something that people do. It takes time, and it's certainly embodied. The answer 'I'm thinking', to the question 'What are you doing?', makes no less sense than the answer 'I'm cooking bolognese sauce.' That one is more visible than the other – because the act of thinking can be visible after a fashion, witness Rodin's famous sculpture – seems to be neither here nor there.

The contrast between meaning and behaviour appears just as problematic when viewed from other directions. How, for example, can human behaviour be oriented predictably towards other humans without at least some shared meanings? *Some* communication is necessary for interaction between humans. And while this case is easy to overstate – I'm reminded of an elegant and intriguing piece in which Alfred Wallace demonstrated mathematically that cognitive sharing isn't necessary for successful interaction[20] – communication must, by definition, depend on establishing a minimum degree of mutual understanding.

This works both ways, of course, as can easily be appreciated by asking whether shared meanings could be established and achieved without established, patterned human interaction. We don't come into the world knowing what we need to know to get by, and we subsequently invent very little of it from scratch.

Although the notion that the human infant is a *tabula rasa* is a massive overstatement, we learn and acquire everything in the course of interaction with others.[21] It isn't a coincidence that human early learning is often referred to as *social*isation.

The distinction between the economic, and the social and the cultural poses similar problems. Ideas such as 'money', 'capital', 'the free market', 'profit' and 'loss', for example, are redolent with political implications, moral values, romance, eroticism, emotional charge, and a host of other complex associations and meanings. And, despite their present, apparently invincible and inevitable, universality, aren't these ideas utterly locally-specific, in terms of time as well as place? In conventional sociological terms, these are socially-constructed cultural products, as indeed is the category of 'the economic' itself. They didn't always exist, and they may at some time in the future cease to make sense. No less than religion or kinship relationships, for example, the production, distribution and consumption of goods – in the context of equally 'cultural' notions of scarcity and surplus – necessarily creates, circulates and transforms meanings, and those meanings are different in different places and at different times.[22]

The 'cultural' and the 'social', and indeed the 'economic', are thus part and parcel of the same phenomenon, the world of humans, going about their everyday business and relating to each other in organised and, at least to some extent, mutually intelligible ways. It is not clear – not to me, anyway – that our capacity to understand that world is improved by carving it up like this. Quite the reverse: as I will argue, these distinctions obscure more than they illuminate.

Culture

Before moving on to the issue raised in the preceding paragraph, some further comments remain to be made about the notion of 'culture'. Returning to the dictionaries, 'culture', too, comes in a range of models and sizes. Perhaps the most predominant in common sense is 'Culture with a capital C': the arts, education, and intellectual achievement. This is often still talked about as synonymous with superior taste and refinement, and in terms of a well-defined hierarchy of life-styles and their worth. It is a matter of distinction.[23] Despite the compensatory notion of 'popular culture' – or, more plausibly perhaps, actually *because* of it[24] – the lower orders are apt to be seen from this point of view as either un-Cultured or, at best, interestingly exotic. This world of the gallery opening, the *avant garde*, the opera, and the literary monthly overlaps – although only partially, and probably uneasily at that – with the self-regarding charmed circle of élite 'society', mentioned earlier.

The development of an exclusive 'Culture with a capital C' is at the heart of those accounts of human history which understand it as a process of social evolution and progress. This gradual journey from brutishness to cultivation receives its clearest sociological examination and articulation in Norbert Elias's discussion of the 'civilizing process' (in which his exposition of the historical and local specificity of understandings of 'culture' and 'civilisation' should be enough to convince anyone of the need for caution in attempting to treat these as analytical categories).[25] The other major sense in which this understanding of 'culture', as art, intellectuality, refinement and sophistication, is reflected within sociology is in the specialist 'sociology of culture', the subject matter of which is still largely defined as 'the arts' – even if the *popular* arts – and the communications media.[26]

More general again, but no less common-sensical, is the use of 'culture' to denote patterns of perceived differences in way of life between different kinds of humans, typically identified in terms of ethnicity, class, or locality. It is a way of talking about group differences, and the observable reality that different groups of humans do things differently from each other in some respects, that they appear to value those differences as markers of belonging and inclusion, and that as a consequence those differences appear to have at least some continuity and pattern over time.[27] In common-sense terms, people are believed to behave differently from each other because their behaviour is determined or proscribed by their 'cultures'. (Although as Weber argued a long time ago, it arguably makes better sociological sense to argue that their 'cultures' are regarded as different, by themselves and others, because they do things differently.[28]) To revisit the discussion of disciplinary boundaries in the previous chapter, this, with a leavening of 'capital C Culture', is the subject matter of cultural studies.

'Culture' can also be defined in opposition to 'nature'.[29] 'Culture' is definitively artificial, the product and achievement of human beings. Returning to the long human passage from brutishness to civilisation, 'culture' thus represents a rising above our natural instincts, the transcendence of our nature. In this sense, 'human nature' is typically understood as the opposite of 'culture'. I will return to this issue in Chapter 6, when I argue that the imperative and irresistible human capacity for 'culture' is, in fact, right at the heart of human nature.

In a related move, 'culture' can also be defined as whatever it is that marks the difference between humans and animals: humans have 'culture', animals do not (although the jury is still out on some primates and cetaceans). The basis of 'culture' in this sense is language and complex communication: the ability to symbolise that which is not there in the immediate present, and to manipulate those symbols. It has been further argued, by anthropologists such as Meyer Fortes and Claude Lévi-Strauss,[30] that the *real* essence of 'culture' can be identified in human kinship relations and reproductive behaviour, specifically in the incest prohibition, which creates a fundamental requirement to go beyond the immediate group and establish co-operative relations and extended communication between human collectivities (not, note, between individuals).

Since these capacities do not come naturally – they are not instinctive, although the *capacity* to acquire them is clearly natural to the species – everything has to be learned as part of the process of individual human development. Most of what we know, we have, in the first instance, to be taught. It is a broadly related point, albeit perhaps obscure, that the word 'culture' as it features in agri*culture*, vini*culture*, the growth of a *culture* in the biology lab, and so on, denotes a <u>complex of meanings</u> that combines, on the one hand, the <u>growth and development</u> which results from the deliberate, <u>nurturing intervention of humans,</u> with, on the other, <u>guiding, shaping, and controlling nature.</u>

Finally, and encompassing all of the above, there is the famous omnibus anthropological definition of 'culture' offered by Edward Tylor in the nineteenth century.[31] Here 'culture' is simply everything that humans do and make. It is every aspect of human life and endeavour: from language to tin openers, roadside hovels to Beethoven, nuclear weapons to money, sexual behaviour to religion, aeroplanes to vulgar childhood rhymes. The list is, literally, endless. Toilet hygiene is no less 'cultural' than Aristotle. This understanding of 'culture' – which remains an important foundation of the anthropological ontology of the human world – sits quite comfortably alongside an understanding of the world of humans as split up into different 'cultures'.

Leaving to one side 'Culture with a capital C' – other than as a common-sense ideology which is as appropriate for our sociological attention as any other ideology – it is possible to pick out a number of common themes which run through the above definitions of 'culture':

- first, 'culture' is definitively human, it is the characteristic way that humans do things, rooted in our capacity for complex communication and reflexive relationships;
- second, it carries within it implications of controlled development and change: 'culture' is, if you like, the medium within which human individuals grow and become competent; and
- third, 'culture' is also a matter of differentiating human collectivities, and their characteristic patterns of behaviour, one from another.

Society and Culture

Like 'society', the concept of 'culture' makes both common sense and sociological sense. The similarities between them do not stop there, however. Looking at them side by side, the notions of 'society' and 'culture' are clearly addressing some of the same concerns:

- 'society' and 'culture' are both ways of talking about the more-than-the-sum-of-the-parts that is the elusive reality of the human world;
- 'society' and 'culture' both evoke bounded human collectivities, which are understood as different from each other; and
- 'society' and 'culture' both refer to humans' established, organised ways of doing things.

The dividing line between 'society' and 'culture' is further obscured if we recognise that ordered social life is impossible without at least some shared meanings, and that the notion of shared meanings makes absolutely no sense other than in the context of interaction. Perhaps the best thing we can do is to propose that the distinction between 'society' and 'culture' is merely a useful heuristic device which helps us to think about and investigate the complexities of the human world, but which doesn't necessarily mean that the human world is actually split into distinct domains in this way.

I'm not, however, convinced by this argument. I can't see any pragmatic sociological necessity for a distinction between 'society' and 'culture'. It enables us to do nothing that we couldn't do just as comfortably, just as plausibly, just as effectively, in its absence. Sociology can do well enough without it. The common-sensical distinction between 'society' and 'culture' is, of course, an appropriate object of sociological analysis – after all, why *do* we make this distinction? And do *all* humans make such a distinction? But that doesn't oblige us to make of it a theoretical proposition or an analytical tool. In fact, if we want to be able to problematise the distinction properly, or understand it better, we probably ought to ditch it.

It isn't just a matter of getting rid of a redundant conceptual distinction, either. There is more at stake. It isn't just that we could do perfectly well without separate concepts of 'society' and 'culture'. My argument is that we would do *better* without them. These concepts actively undermine our understanding of the human world, obscuring the view in at least four senses.

The first of these distortions – if that isn't too bold a word to use – is the violence offered to the integrity of the human world by this conceptual distinction, its *de facto* denial of interconnectedness and messy complexity. To revisit an argument that I outlined earlier, the human world doesn't actually seem to be divided up into 'society' and 'culture'. As is implied by the substantial overlaps in the words' meanings, this is a cleavage in the world of human experience for which there is little or no real evidence. The uses of 'society' and 'culture' as everyday common-sense constructs, the meanings of which are multiplex and imprecise, is one thing; installing them as central elements of our sociological ontology of the human world is quite another.

That the distinction between 'society' and 'culture' is out of kilter with observable realities is further evidence to suggest that our grip on those realities has become subordinated to the demands of intellectual and academic administration. At best, it might be thought to be the tail wagging the dog, that our analytical images of the human world mean more to us than what really goes on in that world. My complaint here isn't that the complex is rendered more simple – that is, of course, an inevitable part of making sociological sense – but that the relationship between sociological sense and the observable realities of the human world has become more tenuous than is necessary or defensible. In Bourdieu's memorable words, the 'reality of the model' has become the 'model of reality'.[32]

The second sense in which the 'society' and 'culture' concepts compromise our understanding of the human world is that they encourage us to take human individuals for granted, as more clear-cut and straightforward than they are. Conventionally, 'society' and 'culture' stand opposed to 'the individual', and as sociologists we tend to talk about individuals rather commonsensically, as if everyone knows what they are: obvious, concrete, *there*. But what is a human individual? A free-standing entity, meaningfully imaginable in isolation? A physical body, certainly, but what else? What is the status of that embodiment, of the blood, the tissue and the bones?

These aren't easy questions. The beginnings of an answer to them can be found, however, in the observation that, apart from the individual three-dimensional physiology of embodiment – in which humans don't differ from other animals – everything else that we recognise as distinctive about human beings is thoroughly embedded in a network of relationships *between* individuals. The body may indeed be the time–space co-ordinates of selfhood, and selfhood the individual, embodied point of view on the world, but as George Herbert Mead argued[33] – and as even Sigmund Freud can be interpreted to say[34] – that individual point of view is always the product of intensive long-term interaction with others. It cannot be understood outside of those networks.

To stay with Mead, and to bring into the discussion other authors, such as Gregory Bateson[35] and Rom Harré,[36] even cognition – *mind* – can sensibly, perhaps even most sensibly, be understood as an interactive phenomenon, impossible to localise exclusively in individual embodiment (and no less impossible to localise collectively, in either 'society' or 'culture'). For example, these words, localised as they are on this page, are an expression of (my) mind – which is a process, not a thing, and not to be confused with my brain – but they don't make sense without (your) mind receiving and interpreting them, in anti-cipation of which they were written. Each entails, and is in some sense entailed *in*, the other (and Freud, Mead, and Bateson, dead as they are, live on in mind: my mind and yours).

All of which suggests that we probably talk too glibly about individuals, and *the* individual. Recognising this, however, we have to be careful. Attending to the observable realities of the human world means that we can't afford to neglect the distinctiveness of human individuals, or the embodiment of individuality. A *pragmatic individualism* is unavoidable if we are to do empirical research.[37] Furthermore, if we need to ground sociological sense in those observable realities – and we do – this must involve respect for, and a relationship to, common sense.

However, for all these reasons, we need to beware of thought-lessly importing the necessary certainties and taken-for-granted-ness of common sense – such as a model of the individual which stops at the skin – into the heart of sociology.

We make a similar mistake about collectivities, which is the third respect in which the concepts of 'society' and 'culture' mislead us. They encourage us to reify collectivities. We talk about collectivities as things, as if – much like individuals – they have mass, density and, above all, skins: real boundaries and definite borders. Several factors come together here, to some of which I have already alluded earlier.

First, as George Lakoff and Mark Johnson have explored so elegantly, metaphor is central to our capacity to model and think about the world at large.[38] For the purposes of this dis-cussion, speaking about phenomena in the world as if they were entities or persons, and the importance of the body as a template for metaphor, are particularly noteworthy. In the human world, these are all especially marked when it comes to how we talk about collectivities: 'The monarchy is *dead* but just doesn't know when to *lie down*'; 'The Stock Exchange took Monday's losses *on the chin*'; 'As the *head* of the family it is my duty to cut the turkey'; 'The *body* of the army advanced across no-man's-land'; 'Playing on the *wing* demands speed, control and unselfishness'; and so on. It seems that Durkheim didn't invent the organic analogy,[39] he just borrowed it from common sense.

Secondly, there is the geo-political constitution of collectivities in the recent modern world. Borders and boundaries – whether they denote private property, municipality, or statehood – are increasingly precisely imagined. The surveyor's theodolite, the border guard's professional suspicion, and the legislator's carefully drafted paragraphs combine to map collectivity onto territory, to render access to territory dependent on citizenship, and to make citizenship among the most consequential arbiters of quality of life.

Finally, there is a long tradition of intellectual discourse – reaching at least as far back as Plato – much of which, in the process of pondering the mysteries of ordered, collective human life, has served to construct it as an object. Perhaps naturally enough, this object became contrasted with its constituent parts, individuals. In sociology this was the dominant organising framework throughout the twentieth century, to the point where it is sociologically unremarkable to talk about 'society' and 'culture' – or 'social structure', for that matter – as affecting individuals, as acting (doing or ensuring this or that), even as having *needs*. The notion of 'culture' is not much different: as Terry Eagleton has recently observed, 'culture' may deny organic determinism but it refuses human autonomy at the same time.[40]

When pressed about our cavalier use of these words, it's my experience that sociologists generally – because some of us, not seeing the problem, do seem to be perfectly content to talk in this way – excuse it as merely shorthand, a handy way of avoiding the need to return to ontological first principles in every argument. While it's possible to have considerable sympathy for this point of view – and it may prove very difficult to turn away from this way of talking – it isn't acceptable. Our shorthand contributes to our misconceptions, and gets in the way of understanding the human world better.

A good and up-to-the-minute example of one such error can be found in John Urry's recent *Sociology Beyond Societies*, in which he argues that in the present and future era of globalisation it no longer makes sense for the basic unit of sociological analysis to be the spatially-bounded set of locally focused institutions that we conventionally refer to as 'a society'.[41] Instead, Urry suggests that sociology must shift its focus, away from boundaries, towards the patterns of mobility of individuals and collectivities, to 'objects, senses, time and space'. In effect, he is saying that there are no more 'societies'.

While I agree with much of this, Urry's argument is, try as he might to avoid it, rooted and imprisoned in the general and long-standing sociological misconception which has always overstated, indeed fundamentally misunderstood, the solidity and boundedness of collectivities. His argument only makes sense if 'societies', in the sense which he is using them as a baseline against which to measure the speed and significance of current changes, are the empirical norm. However, Urry's 'nation-state' – or 'formal organisational' – model of collectivities has never been particularly accurate in terms of the observable realities of the human world. The last two hundred years or so may have witnessed increasingly extensive – and, as I have suggested above, in many respects effective – attempts to firm up and exert control over collective identification and territory, but that doesn't mean that this is an intrinsic feature of the human world. If nothing else, here we have a good example of sociology's need to transcend its modernist assumptions, and hence an argument for generic sociology.

In contrast, an equally long-standing minority analytical tradition – reaching back, through interactionism, as far as Weber, but emerging later, long before postmodernist forays in the same direction, in the anthropological analyses of Fredrik Barth, Jeremy Boissevain, Anthony Cohen, Edmund Leach and others[42] – problematises the solidity and fixity of collective boundaries. The emphasis is on the interactional production and reproduction of collective boundaries during negotiation and symbolisation. Of course, none of these authors is suggesting that there are *no* boundaries; they are, rather, emphasising that the boundaries of human collectivities are permeable, shifting, and problematic. Collectivity is seen as an ongoing practical achievement, and requiring constant attention. In my terms, and rewriting W. I. Thomas's foundational theorem of social constructivism, the fact that collectivities are imagined doesn't mean that they're imaginary.[43]

If this untidy model of the realities of collectivity has any merits, it casts Urry's argument in a different light. First, it means that collectivities – 'societies' – have *never* been neatly bounded, sharply delineated entities. This probably explains, better than anything else, why during recent centuries of population growth and increasing complexity collective projects have become ever more intensive, organised, and controlling; why there has been all this work to establish states as territorially and otherwise stable. While it challenges the state's imaginings of security and

posterity, the current state of collective fluidity correctly identified by Urry is, at most, a variation on a historically routine
theme. It's not intrinsically new. Secondly, viewed in this light
it isn't paradoxical to suggest that 'societies', in Urry's terms,
haven't necessarily become less significant, in terms of either
the observable realities of the human world or the analytical
models of sociologists. Put more positively, sociology should
always have been interested in mobility as well as stability, in
fluidity as well as permanence (not that there's really any such
thing), and in individuals as well as collectivities. Sociology
should always have problematised collectivities.

Finally, and since in some respects this objection is a recasting
of the above in a different light I won't spend too much time
on it, as Harriet Friedmann has recently argued for 'society'[44]
and Terry Eagleton and Adam Kuper for 'culture',[45] these concepts are historical rather than 'objective'. Rooted in Enlightenment reflexivity, and specifically in the linked political projects
of civil society and the nation-state, the sociological notion of
'society', for example, has privileged as universal what is
actually a very particular way of organising the complexities of
human collectivity. It is a revealing example of the routine
ethnocentrism and modernist historicism of sociology's most
basic theoretical apparatus, its ontology of human life. If we are
to escape the thrall of European and North American history, it
is time to find a more general concept to do the job: 'sociology'
and 'culture' will no longer do.

If nothing else, this chapter has been remarkable for my extensive
use of inverted commas. To those readers for whom this has
been tedious, I apologise (and I'll try to be more restrained in
their use in subsequent chapters). Scare quotes on this scale
have been occasioned by my determination not to slip into an
easy naturalisation or acceptance of either 'society' or 'culture'.
Sociologists of all kinds have too widely, and too carelessly,
used both words in ways that overlap too much with their
common-sense usages. More generally, these sociologically

foundational concepts have created two serious theoretical problems.

In the first place, the distinction we draw between 'society' and 'culture' is largely – if not utterly – analytically redundant. The two concepts deal in many respects with the same realities in the human world: the more-than-the-sum-of-the-parts that is the human world, bounded human collectivities, and humans' established, organised ways of doing things. Furthermore, 'society' depends on meaning ('culture') and 'culture' depends on patterned interaction ('society'). The human world is not observably split into separate domains of 'society' and 'culture'.

Secondly, these concepts are misleading in other respects: they smuggle into our thinking an a-sociological, common-sensical understanding of human individuals which opposes them much too sharply to collectivity, and they encourage us, conditioned as we are by the modern practices and institutions of statehood, to reify collectivities and their boundaries into something more clear-cut and definite than they are. Each of these problems is the mirror image of the other, each reinforces the other, and each stands in the way of a better understanding of the human world.

These things taken together constitute a powerful argument for – as a bare minimum – caution and economy in our continued use of the notions of 'society' and 'culture'. This is the foundation for my formulation of an alternative, in the notion of 'the human world' which I will explore further in the next chapter.

Four
The Human World

I have argued in the previous chapter that 'society' and 'culture' are different ways of talking about the same reality: the world of humans, living together as individual members of various collectivities. As concepts, society and culture are not even all that different. If, in the absence of reliable instinctive behaviour patterns, individual humans are to come together collectively (*society*), there needs to be some way of ensuring minimal predictability in interaction. This necessitates that they be socialised into at least a modicum of shared meanings and means of communication (*culture*). Thus to talk about the patterned, organised collective behaviour that we think of as society is necessarily to imply the knowledge, techniques, and values we normally think of as culture. Similarly, to talk about different cultures implies that they have social institutions, memberships and boundaries. And so on.

So, society and culture are alternative ways of talking about the fact that in human collectivity there is something to be found that is more-than-the-sum-of-the-parts. About the fact that human beings do not live any part of their lives as individual isolates. About the inadequacy of arithmetic as an approach to understanding human life. About the fact we do not live in, or construct, a human world of 'just individuals'. About the fact that the notion of 'just individuals' does not, in fact, make much sense. About the fact that there is something else, something more. It may often seem to be elusive, but there is such a thing as whatever it is that is called 'society' and/or 'culture', depending on your point of view and your choice of words.

The Human World

If the arguments of the previous chapter are even close to being right, they suggest that 'society' and 'culture' are not words in which we should have much confidence. They certainly don't appear to get us very far analytically. We need a new way to talk about whatever it is that is more-than-the-sum-of-the-parts, a way of talking which is accompanied by less intellectual and other baggage.

Which is where my preferred alternatives, 'the human world' or 'the world of humans', come into the picture. These synonymous expressions refer, simply, to the world with humans in it, the world that is made by humans, the world as seen from a human point of view. They refer to a world peopled in the first place by individuals, but only and always doing things collectively, with other humans, and always identified, at least in large part, by their collective attachments to other humans. The individual and the collective always co-exist in this conception of the human world, they are not opposites in any sense. It is in this sense that my framework differs most markedly from Schutz's notion of 'the life-world', which is perhaps too resolutely centred on individuals.[1]

Replacing 'society' and 'culture' with 'the human world' removes some of the problems discussed in the previous chapter. Talking about the human world does not, for example, entail adopting problematic distinctions between the social and the cultural (or the economic, the political, or whatever). This allows us to side-step the temptation to prioritise one or the other in terms of their significance or perceived influence. In addition, these expressions place humans unambiguously at the centre of the sociological enterprise. This is a deliberate attempt to avoid reifying the more-than-the-sum-of-the-parts as something 'over and against' individuals, acting on them, existing above their heads or behind their backs. Unlike society and culture, which are definitively collective notions – and therefore also somewhat abstract into the bargain – the human world, while necessarily invoking collectivity, explicitly recognises real individuals, albeit in the plural, in all their concrete, embodied humanity.

To talk about 'the human world' is, therefore, to stress the collective presence of humans as active agents, interacting and intervening in that world. It's a move away from the potential stasis of models of system and structure, towards an axiomatic acceptance of possibility, change and fluidity as routine in human experience. So, although what I am calling 'the human world' is not reducible to embodied individuals, it is constituted of, in and by them. It is emphatically not to be understood as a 'level' of reality that is somehow removed from everyday life.

As a bonus, this notion of 'the human world' allows us to include within our sociological point of view not only the cumulative material presence of the human assembly of technology and artefacts, but also the 'natural world'. While the 'natural world' and the 'human world' are not the same thing, they are different perspectives on the same thing: the world – potentially the entire cosmos as it's known to humans – in which we find ourselves. The human and the natural worlds overlap: the human world is spatially, and in other senses, a zone of the natural world.

In their embodiment humans are 'natural' organisms. Through their activities in the world they shape and reshape everything with which they come into contact, and that feeds back into the human world. The natural world is the universe of constraint and enablement within which the human world exists. If sociology wants to understand one, it must at least deal with the other. Furthermore, the 'natural world' – *as a concept* – is every bit a product of the human imagination, and is a human point of view on the world.[2] In this respect, therefore, one further advantage of the approach and terminology that I am proposing – 'the human world' – is that it can potentially incorporate into the fundamental subject matter of sociology a multi-directional, ecological relationship between humans and their non-human environment. I will return to this in Chapter Six.

Adopting this terminology across the board is unlikely to be straightforward, however. For a start, neither 'the human world' nor 'the world of humans' are particularly elegant: their overuse might easily become clumsy and tiresome. What's more, as

I will explore shortly, there will always be some scope for the specifically sociological use of words such as 'social' or 'cultural'. Finally, even if this were not so, these words – and the concepts of 'society' and 'culture' – are sociologically entrenched to the point where dramatic change would be, at least, an uphill struggle against the inertia of several generations of established habit. Their total banishment therefore seems to be unlikely, unnecessary, and probably unhelpful.

Bearing this in mind, here are a few simple terminological proposals that are intended to move the matter forward without too much fuss. Fundamentally, instead of talking about 'society', or 'culture', I am suggesting that we should refer to the basic, general subject matter of generic sociology as the 'human world' – or the 'world of humans' – as defined above. Adopting this form of words does not require us to be inflexible, however. We will probably, for example, have little choice but to continue talking about this or that 'social world', if we want to be able to capture the distinctive specificity of local arenas of human life. Similarly, and particularly in terms of ethnicity, for example, it's always going to make some sociological sense to talk, where necessary, and even if fairly loosely, about 'different cultures'. If we don't maintain options of this kind, we risk cutting ourselves off so completely from everyday language that our ability to communicate with the widest possible audience would suffer.

Staying with the basics, the absolute importance to humans of relationships with, and the company of, other people, is always going to require sociological emphasis. Hence expressions such as 'sociality', 'social action' and 'social identity' will continue to retain some of their usefulness. Similarly, if we wish to emphasise that the human world is the product of human endeavour, open to human intervention, invested with meaning by humans, and patterned and organised by and because of this, it's difficult to imagine how one could easily or concisely avoid the occasional use of expressions such as 'social construction' and 'cultural construction', or 'social change' and 'cultural change'.

'Culture' itself poses a different problem. One of its most pervasive common-sense meanings – as the élite world of the arts and intellectual activities, Culture with a capital C – organises and legitimates significant institutional arenas and practices in the modern human world. It has thus been taken on board by sociology as a legitimate specialism, the 'sociology of culture', and provides the *raison d'être* for a good deal of cultural studies. If we are to stay in proper touch with the people whose works and doings are our subject matter, this is something else that it is difficult to imagine changing.

In many cases, however, simply dropping a problematic word should be sufficient. For example, it generally adds nothing, in the context of a sociological discussion, to say 'social institution' rather than 'institution', 'social interaction' rather than 'interaction', or to talk about the 'social organisation' of this or that rather than its 'organisation'. Losing these redundancies would merely free up some space in the word count. Finally, allowing for all of the above the points, we should wherever possible substitute 'collective' for those uses of 'cultural' and 'social' which simply denote anything done or held in common, in fairly organised ways, over time, by numbers of humans.

These suggestions are offered in a pragmatic attempt to salvage the baby of mutually-accepted sociological language from the bath-water in which I have been attempting to scrub away the worst excesses inspired by the misleading distinction between society and culture. As I hope is apparent from my attempt to practise what I preach in this book so far, it's neither dramatic nor terribly awkward. It can be boiled down to the following:

- the 'human world' denotes the realm of human experience, practice and organisation in which sociology is interested;
- wherever possible, we should avoid the words 'culture', 'society', and their associated adjectives and adverbs;
- if a replacement for 'cultural' or 'social' is needed, variations on the 'collective' theme will often do quite nicely; and
- where appropriate – as occasionally in this text – we should not be afraid to retain helpful existing usages, particularly if

they facilitate easier and clearer communication with non-sociological audiences.

One of my purposes in writing this book is to demonstrate that this scheme is sufficiently useful and user-friendly to have a future. In talking about the human world throughout, the proof of this particular pudding will be in the eating.

Individuals, Interaction and Institutions

The human world encompasses both individuals and collectivities, with neither category of human phenomena understood as more significant than the other. The relationship between the individual and the collective within this framework can be illustrated by looking at identification and identity.[3] Endlessly talked about, although much less often seriously problematised – the question 'How does identification *work*?' is worth asking over and over again – identification in this context refers to how we humans know who we are, and how we know who others are. Identity is, definitively, a process, which is why it is perhaps more appropriate to talk about identification. As a process, identification is changeable and flexible, although not infinitely so. Identification is simultaneously a matter of behaviour (what humans do) and of how that is understood by ourselves and others (meaning), which is another illustration of the futility of distinguishing between the 'social' and the 'cultural'.

The human world would be an implausible enterprise, and an impossible place to *be*, without some working sense of who we are and who others are. If for no other reason, identity is thus a key concept for sociology. It is also particularly important, however, because there are so few fundamental sociological concepts that comfortably encompass in one notion the collective and the individual. It makes perfect sense to talk about identification as either a collective or an individual phenomenon. What's more, to talk about identity is necessarily to talk about self and others in the same breath. Identification is never just a matter of self-determination, it always involves how others identify me or us, and how I or we identify them. A wholly privatised, unilateral identity is unlikely to the point of impossibility (or delusion). In the first place, the symbolisation and language which are basic to identification are necessarily shared with others in the human world. In the second, as Erving Goffman understood,[4] before an individual identification becomes a reality in the human world other people must at least acknowledge it – and ideally accept or validate it – during interaction. While identification constitutes individuals as individuals – in the eyes of themselves and others – there are no solely individual identifications. Such a notion is a contradiction in terms.

To identify anything – whether it be a sub-atomic particle, a nation, or a galaxy – is to say what it is like (similarity) and what it is unlike (difference). These are the basic elements of identification: there cannot be one without the other. As soon as we say what something is similar to, we also at least imply a universe of things from which it differs. So it is, too, with human identification. To talk about identity is simultaneously to talk about the unique and the shared, the particular and the general. Individual identity may be more a matter of difference – personal uniqueness – while collective identity more a matter of similarity – what the members of the collectivity have in common – but this is only ever a matter of relative emphasis. Individual uniqueness is always, at least in part, constituted in a personally-distinctive portfolio of collective memberships, while collectivities are always differentiated in various respects from other collectivities.

From this point of view, identified, embodied individuals are absolutely central to any sociological understanding of the human world, no less than collective identifications in the shape of groups and categories. Allowing for this, what kind of analytical framework do we need in order to bring together the collective and the individual without losing sight of one in the shadow of the other? One way to approach this question, which I introduced in Chapter One, is to think about the human world as three different 'orders':

- the *individual order* is the human world as made up of embodied individuals, and what-goes-on-in-their-heads;

- the *interaction order* is the human world as constituted in the relationships between individuals, in what–goes–on–between–people; and
- the *institutional order* is the human world of pattern and organisation, of established–ways–of–doing–things.

This notion of the 'order' – borrowed from Erving Goffman,[5] and perhaps less obviously influenced by Anthony Giddens[6] – has been chosen in part because the human world, whatever else it may be, is ordered even if it is not necessarily always orderly. Pattern is part of the observable reality of the human world (although not all pattern is observable by the naked eye). The word 'order' is also, however, intended to emphasise that these are classificatory notions – epistemological devices – which shouldn't be confused with the actual phenomena and localities of the human world to which they refer. They are an act of ordering in their own right – devices for carving up the observable realities of the human world into manageable and meaningful chunks – and thus exist only in the eye of the beholder. Only by sticking firmly to this line can we hope to avoid carelessly reconstituting them as the kind of conceptual reifications which we are seeking to avoid.

The observable realities in question are anything but mysterious: there are embodied individuals, interaction happens, and institutions persist and have a presence in the world. The individual, interactional and institutional orders cannot be said to exist in any of these senses, however. They are *not* observable realities. As analytical concepts, they are designed simply to help us think clearly about the complexities of the human world. They are 'ways of talking' or 'ways of knowing', nothing else. In observable reality, individuals, interaction, and institutions necessarily co-exist, they are not easily separated, and they don't make sense without each other. So although for analytical purposes these 'orders' can be thought of as distinct – and can be talked about in isolation from each other – in observable reality the phenomena about which they help us to think aren't so easily separated. They are a trinity. They necessarily fill the same physical and social spaces:[7] each is based on and in real, embodied individuals, their behaviour and products, and processes of identification are basic to each of them.

To unpack this in a little more detail, let's begin with individuals and what-goes-on-in-their-heads. Identification is basic to how we experience and understand ourselves, in the most personal, private sense: how we *live* as ourselves, how we *be* ourselves, how we relate *to* ourselves. Reflexivity and identification are prerequisites of each other. If we know ourselves, we do so at least in large part in terms of our identities. Without identification it isn't clear to me what there would be to be reflexive *about*. Furthermore, identity is always, either actually or potentially, embodied, in individuals. Even the 'virtual identities' of the internet chat room are well understood by participants to be expressions of embodied persons, each at their keyboard.[8] Without embodied individuals there is no identification.

But individual identity is always constructed in and through interaction with others. This is so in at least four senses. First there is the foundational role of socialisation and learning – whether in early life, or later – in the assumption and rejection of identities. If we do know who we are, it is only because, in the earliest instance, somebody taught us. Secondly, everyday life is a perpetual trial of identification, depending for its success on the routine interactional validation by others of who we are. Thirdly, we should not underestimate the degree to which the imposition of identities on individuals by others – what I have called elsewhere categorisation – is influential in the routine construction of identity.[9] Self-identification, whether individual or collective, is only one side of the coin, and not always the most important. Finally, in an insight which may be the most important lesson that G. H. Mead's work has for us,[10] in order to be able to know ourselves, we have to know others, too: recognising *me* involves recognising *you*.

But if identity is so fundamentally a matter of interaction with others, then, equally, interaction also depends, for much of whatever coherence or transparency it exhibits – much of its *order* – on identification. Without identification of self and others, interaction would be impossible. How would any of us have any idea what to expect from people, without some idea of who they were? Predictability would diminish dramatically. That it is so difficult to imagine a human world without knowing who its members are, is revealing of our absolute reliance on identification.

Identity's capacity for change is also rooted in interaction and negotiation with others (and without that flexibility, interaction and negotiation would be immeasurably more difficult). In this sense, as suggested above, identity should be understood as a perpetual process, as identification. However, all that is solid does not melt into air: some identities are less malleable than others. Rooted as they are either in very early primary socialisation, or in collective understandings of embodiment, identifications such as gender, sexuality, and 'race' may prove to be very resistant to intervention. That they are so stubborn is also in part to do with the power of others – the rest of ego's local human world – who may refuse to validate any changes that an individual attempts in these respects. The human world is definitively multilateral.

This suggests that although all identities, as established ways of doing things, are institutionalised to some degree, some identifications are more institutionalised than others. Institutions are significant, among other reasons, as contexts for the patterned distribution of resources, rewards, and penalties. Identifications are major criteria according to which these are allocated. Furthermore, institutions themselves, whether informal or formal, generate patterns of position or office which exist only in relation to each other: these are identifications, always actually or potentially occupied by individuals. Whether it is a friendship network, a family, a business organisation, or a nation-state, the same holds good for all institutions. Even an institution as ephemeral as, say, a queue to get into a night-club, is structured in terms of identificatory positions – doorman, woman, man, drunk, 'under-age', back-of-the-line, head-of-the-queue, VIP (well, on the guest list, at least), 'you're barred', and so on – which are not randomly allocated, through some of which individuals may progress (or not), and to which are attached differential rewards or penalties.

To judge from the above, it is only possible to separate the individual and the collective – the particular and the general, the biographical and the historical – for analytical and presentational purposes. The observable and experiential realities of the human world suggest that the individual and the collective co-exist in the same space; that, in some sense which has so far proved sociologically elusive, they may not be so different after all.

So far, so good. To say this should not, however, lead us into the mistake of imagining that the individual and the collective are the same. That is not what inseparable means. As I have suggested earlier, in any consideration of the relationship between the individual and the collective, it is immediately striking that individuals are obvious or visible in a way that collectivities aren't. This is pragmatic individualism again: embodied humans are 'there', breathing, moving, and occupying a fairly definite space. Collectivities are not always 'there'; and even when they appear to be, there's a lot more to it than that.

A football club, for example, is a collectively self-conscious group. Its front-line manifestation is 'the team': eleven men – let's stick with professional soccer for the moment, so it is men – 'there' on the pitch, kitted out in uniform, playing eleven other men. But is it then a different team after a substitution or two? Will it still be the same team next year, after transfers, retirements, and new signings? What about the rest of the squad? Are they members of 'the team'? And what about 'the B team', 'the youth team', and so on? What counts as 'the club' is even less straightforward. The coach, the manager, the physio, the ground staff, the boot boys, the administrative staff, the people who work in the club shop, the catering staff, the programme sellers, the board of directors, the shareholders. Where, in that list, does 'the club' begin and end? What about the supporters' club? Unofficial supporters' clubs? The season-ticket holders? The rest of the fans? Retired players? Players' wives, partners, children?

Although this is a simple example, it clarifies and illustrates three important points. First, the boundary of membership of a collectivity is typically not clear. Who belongs is likely to be situational – for some purposes the wives and partners will be 'in', for example, but not for others – and thus, to an extent, manipulable and vulnerable to the needs of the moment. The embodied boundary of an individual human is, by contrast, fairly straightforward. Although this doesn't mean that the nature of individuality is either straightforward or exhaustively defined by the boundaries of embodiment, the contours of the epidermis are, if nothing else, clear. Collectivities, however, do not have skins in this sense.

Secondly, collectivities persist despite the coming and going of their individual members due to birth, volunteering, capture, resignation, expulsion, or death. What is more, there is a sense in which, under the right circumstances, collectivities can be revived, brought back from the dead, so to speak (witness the post-1989 re-constitution of the Balkans and Eastern Europe, or the resurrection on the concert stage of The Velvet Underground, a few year later). Under the present constraints of medical science, however, individuals are very different: the human life-span may be indeterminate, within limits, but it is much more definite.

That collectivities endure in ways that their constituent human members cannot, suggests, finally, that there is something quite specific about collectivities, and about the way that they are conjured up and imagined. Something that transcends and survives change of all kinds and degrees. In the case of a football club, this includes a wide range of stuff:

- there is the ground, the stadium, and its associations (imagine Spurs without White Hart Lane, for example, or, in an example that's rousing the fans' wrath at the time of writing, Wimbledon moving to Milton Keynes);
- the club badge and colours are enormously significant, even in an era in which the more successful and commercially acute clubs boast three or four heavily merchandised, very expensive, home and away strips;

- clubs have nick-names (and as in the case of West Bromwich Albion, for example, they can have more than one: in addition to their obvious abbreviated nick-name, West Brom, they are also called 'the Throstles' and 'the Baggies');
- there may be silverware in the trophy cases, although success in this respect is not necessary (indeed, the consistency of adversity can have its own solidary effect);
- clubs have their myths, legends and histories (Manchester United, for example, has the tragedy of the 'Busby babes' and the Munich disaster, and the triumph of the 1968 European Cup final);
- supporters have their own organisation within the organisation, the supporters' club, which may have many branches, nationally and internationally (as in the case of Man United and Glasgow Rangers, for example);
- supporters have their own songs (Liverpool has 'You'll Never Walk Alone', West Ham, 'I'm Forever Blowing Bubbles', and so on);
- supporters also share in a detailed and arcane body of knowledge, embodied in collective oral tradition, which can stretch back many years, of who – players and supporters – did what, when and where;
- clubs may have a supporter base that's related to local communal identifications (as in the sectarian histories of Rangers and Celtic in Glasgow, or the rivalry in Sheffield between The Owls and The Blades);
- supporters often have their own unofficial organisations, ranging from 'alternative' fanzines, to organised teams of hooligans;[11]
- participation in national and international networks of affiliation, such as associations and leagues, creates clubs as corporate bodies with relationships with other clubs, and organises the matches in which clubs necessarily actualise themselves;
- legal incorporation matters, and is embodied in the relevant documents; and, finally,
- even the financial accounts are significant, because soccer is, after all, a business.

These are not intangibles. Some of them are *very* tangible, and they are all the sometime products of people, which require at least some maintenance work by other people if they are to persist and prosper. Nor are they fixed: it's one thing to persist, quite another to be set in concrete, or be immune from catastrophe: it is not unheard of for clubs to disappear altogether, and, as the example of Rushden and Diamonds has recently shown, new clubs can appear from the ashes. Be that as it may, taking all of the above together, they amount to something more-than-the-sum-of-their-parts; something of which only aspects can ever be visible at any one time, or from any one point of view (although this ineffable collectivity can more easily be *felt* on the right occasion). They symbolise the club. In an important sense they *are* the club, in a way that its members at any one time are not, and cannot be.

This example illustrates the potential value of the basic model of the human world – as the individual order, the interaction order, and the institutional order – proposed earlier. The club exists in individuals, in interaction (people doing things), and in institutions (established ways of doing things). In fact, it *is* an institution (and a complex of constituent institutions). But not all institutions are real live groups (so to speak). The collectivity of group-ness is only achieved when the individual, the interactional, and the institutional come together under a symbolic umbrella that conjures them up as something other, something new, something sufficiently multi-faceted to allow a diversity of members to identify with it, emotionally as well as cognitively, without any disabling necessity for strict conformity or consensus. Something, in other words, more-than-the-sum-of-its-constituent-parts. Something, perhaps, a little mysterious.

Understanding Change

The definitive persistence-in-change of collectivities brings me face to face with the other basic sociological theme: our understanding of how, and why, the human world changes. There are essentially three established ways of understanding change in and of the world of humans. First, the actions of people – whether individually or collectively, whether deliberately or unintentionally – are believed to be what causes or inhibits change. Secondly, change is understood to be a consequence, or not, of the characteristics and dynamics of 'society' or 'culture', understood as impersonal social structures or systems. Thirdly, change is said to come from outside 'society' or 'culture': it is a result of the impact on the human world of environmental factors such as pestilence, climate change, and so on.

The third can be ignored for the moment, since it's neither a comprehensive model of change in itself, nor definitively sociological. It recognises that we humans don't live our lives in a socio-cultural bubble, and that the environment regularly deals us hands which disrupt our routine, taken-for-granted lives. This is most useful, given my arguments in Chapter Six that the human world and the natural world can fruitfully be understood as deeply and reciprocally implicated in each other. However, it doesn't say anything more interesting about change than that.

The other two models of change are more to the point of the present discussion. On the face of it, understanding change as the product of human action fits in well with the vision of the human world I am proposing here. Although it fits, however, it doesn't necessarily do so in a straightforward way. In the first place, to talk about change at all can mislead us into thinking that change is a departure from a normal, steady state of affairs, thus: original state, followed by human intervention or action or happening, followed by result ... change to new state. However, the human world is never static. We may prefer to think of it as ordered and predictable, and we may invest time and effort in trying to render it so, but movement and transformation are of its routine essence.

Movement and transformation are not necessarily the same thing, however. During their dealings with each other, individuals do all kinds of things. Some of these will appear to support the usual or 'normal' state of affairs, some to ignore it, some to reject it, and some to modify it. All actions are movement – process, if you'd prefer – and which will produce change is not necessarily clear at the time. That depends, at least in large part, on other people: whether they recognise what is happening, and how they respond to it. For change to occur, old ways of doing things have to be stopped and/or new ways of doing things have to become established and recognised. In other words, change frequently involves institutionalisation (which, only apparently paradoxically, involves, certainly in the first instance, the inhibition of further change). Here again there are the observable realities of individuals, interaction, and institutions, bound up with each other.

But there are other matters to be considered too. Perhaps the most well-worn issue here – capable of generating a great deal more heat than light – is the question of whether human action should be interpreted as being the result of rational calculation,[12] or as something else: as the product of habit,[13] as an expression of 'social structural' factors such as class or generation,[14] or perhaps as the result of more-or-less unconscious psychological impulses and drives.[15] With respect to the latter, it's necessary to recognise the influence on human behaviour of the emotions in all their complexity: Weber and Durkheim, for example, were both correct to do so.[16] It is also necessary to emphasise the social constructedness and cultural variability of emotions.[17] However, for sociological purposes I'd want to rule out immediately explanatory recourse to something called 'the unconscious'. Not because it doesn't exist, but because I can't see any way in which it can be *shown* to exist. It may be possible to overlook this problem if one is concerned with psychoanalysis as a therapeutic dialogue, or an interesting metaphysic, but it can't be overlooked if we're doing sociology.

Structural determination is no less problematic as an explanation of human behaviour. The basic difficulty can be summed up somewhat brutally in the question, what *is* social structure? There are three possible answers. First, in the best traditions of the 'society' concept, structure might be a transcendent reality which exists over our heads or behind our backs, in which case the objection is similar to the case against the unconscious: how could we establish its existence? What's more, even if we could establish its existence, what kinds of mechanisms could possibly connect it to individual human actions? Secondly, structure might simply be a metaphor – a way of talking about the pattern and order of the human world for the analytical purposes of sociology – in which case it surely can't determine, or even influence, anything (other than the behaviour of any sociologists and others whose actions and conduct, unlikely and sad as it sounds, might be informed by the notion[18]). Finally, in realist terms we could regard structure as simply the existing observable phenomena of the human world – human actions and their products, i.e. individuals, interaction and institutions – under the mutual constraints of which humans routinely act. In which case, neither determination nor causation are appropriate notions if tautology is to be avoided.

This leaves as the motors of human behaviour a decidedly Weberian portfolio of the emotions, conscious decision-making (informed by a range of rationalities, from the traditional to the scientific) and habit.[19] These are all obvious influences on human behaviour. But so, however, is compulsion, the exercise of unadorned power in all of its many guises.[20] The ability of others to bend us to their will is difficult to distinguish from decision-making or habit – because submitting to compulsion is, after all, often a decision of a sort, and it can become established as habit (as in much effective socialisation) – but I think it's important to do so. Doing something because your emotions impel you to it, doing something because you want to, in whatever way or for whatever reason, doing something thoughtlessly, because that's what has always been done, and doing something because you perceive someone else to have foreclosed the alternatives, are four very different states of affairs in the human world, and they are generally recognised as such. These are distinctions that are worth maintaining.

So, there are many causes of and reasons for what people do, and all human behaviour *can* result in change. Whether any specific deed *will* prove to be transformative, however, isn't necessarily obvious, to participants or to watching sociologists. In the most trivial – or is it the most profound? – sense all behaviour alters the human world in some respect. So do all happenings in the natural world. As Stephen Jay Gould and others interested in the very long term have argued so persuasively, the contingency of small events is the stuff of the large patterns of history and evolution.[21] Complexity and chaos produce pattern and order, and who can predict what will happen down the line after a butterfly stamps its foot? Indeed... but I am concerned here with humans rather than butterflies, and with transformation rather than routine motion. Change in the world of humans does not simply mean alteration: it is alteration that is noticed and recognised as significant by the people concerned. It is alteration to which human meaning is attached.

The key sociological point in this respect was recognised by Max Weber.[22] Humans have their intentions and projects – they certainly have their reasons – and these are undoubtedly influential in the scheme of things: they make things happen. But *what* they make happen, and *how*, and the relationship between objectives and outcomes, none of these are necessarily predictable. Even if we do know motives and reasons – for they are often obscure – they don't explain everything. Even when we think about it – because often we don't – we can rarely be confident about the outcomes of what we do ourselves. The human world is, to a significant degree, realised and transformed in the unintended consequences of human behaviour.

Much change, perhaps even most change in the human world, is, therefore, a complex and cumulative process in which small events can prove to have significant consequences, while large events may turn out to be historically relatively unimportant. Change can appear to 'just happen', or to be pre-destined or otherwise mysterious. We tell ourselves that 'things are out of our hands', 'there's nothing to be done', 'that working people don't have a chance', 'that accidents will happen', or whatever. Explanations can be sought in the supernatural realm, in notions of chance or fate, in the evil power of top-hatted capitalists, or, if you're a certain kind of sociologist, in social forces, systems, and structures.

The Ontology of Collectivity

The sentence immediately above returns the discussion to the ontological complexities that surround the more-than-the-sum-of-the-parts: the vexed questions of 'society' and 'culture'. On the one hand, the observable world of embodied individual humans and their artefacts is, in an important and real sense which shouldn't be dismissed out of hand, 'all there is'. On the other, however, there is a persistent, very human, nagging sense that there *is* something-more-than-the-sum-of-the-parts.

This sense is, of course, one reason why explanations of social change which invoke 'societal dynamics', or the interaction of 'systems', 'forces' and 'structures', have proved so attractive, to so many people. However, while a sense of collective reality is enormously important – indeed, it is in many respects what has inspired me to write this book – it can also lead us into difficulties. On the one hand, systems models and notions of structure have shown themselves, over and over again, to be more amenable to statics (the reproduction of the human world) than to dynamics (the production of the human world). On the other, they are grist *par excellence* to the mill of free-floating theory, speculation and abstraction undisciplined by systematic inquiry into the observable realities of the human world. So, caught between plague and cholera – to translate a wonderful Danish expression – what is to be done? Are reification and over-abstraction the unavoidable, if perhaps unintentional, consequences of maintaining a sense of the more-than-the-sum-of-the-parts?

I don't think so. It is possible to look at the observable realities of the human world and to discern, in different ways, the immanent 'more-ness' of collectivity revealed in the practices of everyday life. I want briefly to explore five of these – there are doubtless others – all of which turn out, on closer inspection, to be so implicated and tangled up in each other that it isn't fanciful to think of them as different perspectives on the same phenomenon.

The first is inseparable from the diffuse human sense of collectivity, but isn't in any sense limited to it. It's the inability to accept the visible, physical world of appearances as 'all there is', which I mentioned in the previous chapter and will return to in Chapter Six. It can be found everywhere: from religion, to politics, to science, to everyday romance, to literature. If nothing else, it suggests that Weber was mistaken about the inevitability of the 'disenchantment of the world'.[23] To advance a large claim, what I am talking about here seems to be fundamental to the imaginative powers which are part of our human nature. Without our imaginations – our predilection for enchantment – there would be nothing but ourselves and whoever was in our line of sight at the time. That would be all, and it probably wouldn't even amount to the sum-of-its-individual-parts.

Secondly, and probably fairly obviously, there is identification with others within groups. This is the everyday, concrete collectivity that provides the working model for the ever more abstract collectivities of large-scale corporations and polities. In terms of size, this sense of collectivity stretches from the daily intimacies of family, friendship and love, to the sometimes tenuous identifications that hold together nations or international business organisations. Small or big, however, group identification is not 'essential' or 'primordial' – although the *need* for collectivity appears to be part of our human species-being – and requires continuous maintenance work if it is to prosper.

Which brings me, thirdly, to the shared symbolic universes – borrowing an expression from Berger and Luckmann[24] – that play such a large part in the production and reproduction of identification. Encompassing all of the repertoires of verbal and non-verbal communication, these are perhaps the best arguments for the more-than-the-sum-of-the-parts it's possible to find. Taking language as an example, competent individual language use doesn't depend on being able to explicate its working principles, and no individual language speaker ever knows a language's complete vocabulary (in part because vocabulary is always open and unfinished). To further emphasise the definitive collectivity of language, we necessarily learn language from others, the primary context of language use is communication with others, and linguistic borders are generally indefinite (in that there is overlap, mingling and sharing between language speakers). Language is definitively, and diffusely, more-than-the-sum-of-its-parts.

Fourthly, taking inspiration this time from Simmel's observations on dyads and triads,[25] the difference between two humans interacting and three humans interacting, even if only fleetingly and on a one-off basis, is qualitative, geometry rather than arithmetic. Add the third person, and something different – not just *bigger* – emerges in terms of the strategic and tactical interactional possibilities, the spaces, the inclusions and the exclusions that become available. This is one of the reasons why it's possible to talk about collectivities at all, and why, sociologically, the study of institutions and organisations has proved to be so enduringly fascinating. The whole is definitively more than the sum of the parts: one plus one plus one equals more than three.

Finally, there is something called 'the present'. Despite a well-established philosophical tradition which understands the present as an unstable fugitive zone of perpetual transition between the future and the past,[26] humans successfully – and necessarily – construct a 'present' that is neither ephemeral nor fleeting. The tenses and turns-of-phrase of language, the security of institutional continuity, the solidity of a here-and-now human-made physical environment, and the relative constancy of embodied, identified individuals, all conjure up the present as a time-space which is sufficiently stable, 'real' and workable – sufficiently unproblematic that it can be taken for granted – for human life to proceed. In Mead's words, the present is the 'locus of reality';[27] in mine, it is the locus of the human world. In either, it's more-than-the-sum-of-its-parts.

The transcendence of the visible, the mutualities of group identification, the centrality to human experience of shared symbolism, the geometry of relational form, and the stabilisation of 'the present' as a workable reality, can all be understood individually, interactionally, and institutionally. Taken together they suggest that collectivity may not really be so mysterious. The good news is that there seems to be such a thing as 'society', after all, and it isn't necessarily hard to find. Allowing that without them it would be nothing, the world of humans isn't only a world of individuals.

That the collectivity of the human world can be discovered and perceived – in other words, that it is an observable reality – moves the discussion on to the sociological importance of empirical research. Documenting what humans do 'in the present' and the cumulative patterns of history – which, by the way, is not *just* what people *think* it is, something infinitely relative and constructable – is vital if we are to understand the human world, if we are successfully to theorise social change or the relationship between the individual and the collective. The systematic inquiry that is fundamental to these tasks is the subject of the next chapter.

Five

Exploring the Human World

The title of this chapter reflects a general argument of this book in assuming the existence of observable realities which constitute the human world, realities about which it is possible to find out and say something; assuming, in other words, that there is something to explore. This assumption is the ontological and epistemological basis of our everyday lives, without which we couldn't step outside our front doors with any confidence. In this respect doing sociology is no different from doing other everyday things: without this assumption it is difficult to imagine what sociology would actually be *about*, or what might be the point of undertaking research at all.

Rationales for Research

Accepting that there are, indeed, observable realities is the keystone of the everyday realism which is essential if we are to steer general theory and empirical research back to within hailing distance of each other again. From the perspective of everyday realism, sociology should be an 'empirically responsible' discipline,[1] and by that token, if sociology is worth doing, so is research. However, lest this be misunderstood to suggest that the issues are simple – and research less complicated than, in all respects, it is – it is necessary to begin this discussion by reviewing why sociologists undertake research into (and in) the human world.

First, in much the same way as any other systematic investigators, in the natural sciences or wherever, sociologists undertake research in order to assess the relationship of their theories, their particular ways of making sense of the human world, to that world (or at least they should). Theory and empirical inquiry are inseparable (or at least they should be). Although sociological theory isn't a matter of proof or predictive certainty – if only because humans are too prone to changing their minds, and the epistemological difficulties posed by other human minds too real – there are degrees of greater or lesser fit between sociological theories and observable reality. This is so in two closely related respects. First, the abstraction and generalisation that are central to theorising, and the documentation and discovery of patterns in human behaviour as a result of systematic inquiry, should be mutually dependent. Secondly, theories should be at least open to the discipline offered by the possibility of empirical falsification.[2] Without that discipline, everything and anything becomes sayable, but an important criterion of the sense or nonsense of what's been said vanishes.

In the second place, the nature of human cognition is an important factor. Like all the higher primates, we are incorrigibly inquisitive. Unlike the other higher primates – as far we know, anyway – we are complexly and extensively imaginative. For example, as discussed in another context in the previous chapter, we are arguably impelled to transcend the material world of appearances. Going beyond the visible here-and-now seems simply to be something that humans do. So too is our urge to impose classificatory order on the world: naming and categorising are another aspect of our innate imaginative capacities.[3] Our imaginations are massively definitive of who we are – both as a species and as individuals – and go a long way to explaining why we have invented the -ologies.

This suggests, further, that the role of individual history and experience – which includes political and ethical conviction – in shaping our curiosity, in deciding *which* research gets done and by *whom*, shouldn't be underestimated. If there is a cumulative logic of scientific inquiry which informs sociological research – and I'm not wholly convinced that this notion applies to science, let alone sociology – then it's probably no more important than the biographies and idiosyncrasies of the human beings who plan and execute it. Transplant a boy at the age of eight from middle-class Yorkshire to working-class, sectarian Northern

Ireland and it shouldn't be so surprising that, as in my case, it's the complexities of identification that prove abidingly fascinating. Many sociologists could tell a similar tale.

Next, and not unconnected to theory and curiosity, one of the reasons that we continue to do research is that the world of humans changes, all the time. As I discussed in Chapter Two, it was the nineteenth-century experience of massive social change which called sociology as we know it today into existence. It is a generic characteristic of the human world that new phenomena emerge and existing ones change their meaning. Hence the impossibility of sociological predictive certainty. Hence, too, sociology's need of an up-to-the-minute knowledge base, a consideration which ties research directly in to our teaching role.

This point, however, suggests a number of other observations, not least about the subject matter of sociology and the subject matter of the sciences. In physics, for example, discovery typically involves finding out new stuff about the universe as a consequence of either enhanced technology – better telescopes, for example – or new explanations, as in Einstein's mathematical proofs of relativity. It is generally not because something new has come into existence. It may be stuff that was hitherto unknown to humans, but not actually new (very rarely, anyway).

Sociology is fundamentally different in this respect. Humans are innovators, and the world in which sociologists are interested is regularly transformed. For humans, change is routine. Thus the stuff to which sociologists must attend, and which they must attempt to understand, can be previously known-about; it can be hitherto unknown but not new; or it can actually be *new*. Stone tool technologies, the wheel, irrigation, slavery, the city, metallurgy, the state, writing, mathematics, cavalry, printing, the steam engine, the factory system, democracy, vaccination, sociology, telecommunications, aeroplanes, antibiotics, the contraceptive pill, or the computer on which I am writing this: in every case there was a time when they simply did not exist, and they all opened up previously unimagined possibilities. In the ways in which they were taken up and developed, they all transformed the human world. That world is still, however, the human world, and there is some constancy to be found in humans themselves. Our natures seem to be much slower to change than our institutions or technology. Having invented the internet, for example, humans have chosen shopping, sex, and chat as its most popular uses:[4] hardly world-historical or revolutionary.

In putting the matter thus, I am, of course, overstating the differences between what sociologists do and the work of natural scientists.[5] Biologists, for example, deal with a world in which mutation is routine. This, however, is where the other contrast between sociological research and natural science research makes itself felt: change in the human world doesn't *just happen* (even when it is an unintended consequence of something else), it is the product of self-conscious activity, and spreads via the human capacity for complex communication. This latter is a key to understanding sociological research: not only is change in the human world different from other kinds of change, but we can investigate what's going on by talking to the humans concerned. This means that we are our own subject matter. We do not just undertake research *into* the human world: our research is *in* that world (in a way that an oceanographer, for example, isn't part of the marine environment).

Finally, and apropos sociology being an integral part of the world it studies, there are other, overlapping and perhaps less attractive, reasons for doing research, which apply with equal force to sociologists and natural scientists. We are all under pressure to do research, in education systems in which research achievement is an important criterion determining individual careers and departmental funding. There is peer-group pressure too, the interpersonal dynamics of which are not wholly reducible to institutional factors. In addition, we undertake research because government agencies, charities, business organisations, and so on, offer us money to do so. Contract research puts the bread on the table for some of us, while for others consultancy work buys holidays and cars (as – before anyone says it – can writing books).

So we explore the human world for a range of reasons, from the high-minded to the base. Sometimes we do sociological research, sometimes more mundane social research. At different points in any career the influence of all of the motivations that I have just discussed can be experienced. They can co-exist quite happily, too: intellectual curiosity and single-minded ambition are not, for example, uncommon bedfellows, and it's quite possible to have one's head in the stratosphere *and* feet of clay. Between the significance of biography and standpoint, our membership of the human world, and the pressures and temptations from inside and outside the academy, the pursuit of epistemological objectivity in sociological research is as vulnerable as it is vital.

Observable Realities

To return to observable realities, why do I feel such a need to insist that they exist and can be known? The reason is that sociologists have become interestingly coy about this issue. Not all sociologists, it must be said. Even in the qualitative methodology literature, there is a consistent thread defending moderate versions of realism or positivism,[6] and I suspect that most people who actually do empirical sociological research would, if pushed – and some more spontaneously and enthusiastically – subscribe to one or other of these positions. Too many researchers, however, are content to take the matter wholly for granted. Many others would simply rather not tangle with a powerful anti-positivist orthodoxy in sociology: in qualitative research circles this has achieved the status of public, conventional wisdom and successfully reserved to itself the ethical high ground by claiming empowering and emancipatory virtues such as 'listening to' or 'giving voice to' research subjects.[7]

This orthodoxy rests on the assumption, which probably derives its ultimate intellectual respectability from Kant, that we have no direct-line access to 'reality', whatever that might be. The basic position is that all we have available to us are our own and others' accounts or representations of reality. Questions about ontology and the nature of reality are set to one side and what matters is whose account *counts*, which is a political, rather than an epistemological, issue.

This position has at least four specifically sociological sources and versions. First, social constructionism in all of its hues is often, superficially, understood in this light. This is despite the insistence of Thomas, Berger and Luckmann, and, more recently, Searle that the product of social construction is a 'reality'.[8] Secondly, and closely related, the relativist sociology of knowledge draws its inspiration from Marx's well-known remark that the ruling ideas of any epoch are the ideas of the ruling class.[9] Thirdly, the 'literary turn' in anthropology has encouraged some ethnographers in the belief that they are merely writers of accounts, for which they can claim no special authority: all we can ever aspire to from this point of view is a proliferation of 'representations'.[10] Sociology is no more factual, from this point of view, than fiction. Finally, the relativist thrust of postmodernism and its fellow travellers, in rejecting grand historical narratives and the epistemological authority of Enlightenment rationalism, has been inexorably in the same direction.[11]

Before addressing the failure of epistemological nerve which has resulted from all this, it is worth saying that I will be doing so as an unapologetic social constructionist, who appreciates the potential authority of fiction – novelists are often subtle and trustworthy ethnographers – who applauded the toppling of Progress from its pedestal, and for whom Kantian rationalism is, as we shall see, infinitely preferable to naïve empiricism. None the less, going along with the insistence that the only end products to which we can aspire are differing, but equally valid, accounts or representations of the human world has led sociology into a muddle. A muddle in which too much research, rather than being 'about' whatever it is that it definitely *is* about, evades its responsibilities by exploring 'issues around' its topic. A muddle in which empathy or self-absorbed reflexivity are substituted for epistemological rigour. A muddle in which some qualitative research, in particular, has become unsystematic and superficial to the point that it would shame decent journalism.

Central to this muddle is the intimidatory profundity which has been allowed to gather, like a fairy-tale hedge of thorns, around epistemology. Partly due to its other life as a branch of scholastic philosophy,[12] and partly due to the prolix navel-gazing that has, for several decades now, been the reflexive norm for too many social theorists, the very word 'epistemology' is capable of striking terror into the hearts of professionals and students alike. This is a pity. From a practical research point of view, epistemology isn't necessarily complicated, and it is important. Nor are the practicalities of epistemology confined to research. In our everyday lives, we regularly ask questions about knowledge and knowledge claims, and we do so without being intimidated. We have to, in order to get by.

At its least frightening, epistemology is simply discourse – talk – about knowledge, and how we know what we claim to know. Its key questions are relatively clear-cut, such as 'What do I have to do to find out about X?' or 'What is her basis for claiming to know about Y?' If an old friend, for example, telephones you to tell you that your mutual acquaintance so-and-so is having an affair with such-and-such, one of the first questions you are likely to ask, if you're sensible anyway, is how he's come to know this, and what the status of the information is. When a politician in an interview asserts that most people want 'sensible' immigration laws, one of the first things you ought to ask yourself is how she knows that. When a coalition of Christian fundamentalists, psychotherapists, and social workers tell us that our children are threatened by an underground conspiracy of ritual or satanic abusers, before responding we have a responsibility to ask them to show us the evidence, and to ask searching questions about its status.[13] And when Anthony Giddens, for example, tells us that reflexive self-identity is a distinctively modern phenomenon, the same scepticism, and the same questions, are in order.[14]

While the practical epistemologies of research and everyday life may be pretty much the same, our responses to them are not. This is one crucial respect in which research differs from other kinds of 'finding out' and knowing, and it's where method and system assume their importance. As I have already suggested in Chapter One, in this sense we can think about methodology – the discourse about research methods, their appropriateness, their advantages and shortcomings, their ethics, and the nature of the data they produce – as *systematic applied epistemology*. It's about what we have to do in order to be able to make defensible knowledge claims; it's about why sociological sense can compete with common sense.

Among the methodological issues raised by 'observable reality' are whether the world can be investigated by method alone, and the place of theory in the process of knowing. These questions lie at the heart of a long-standing disharmony within the philosophy of science. The *empiricist* standpoint views the world as 'there' and available for inspection, ready to be apprehended via experience and sensory perception. What matters is the power and precision of our techniques for investigating the world. Put quite as crudely as this, empiricism is probably a minority position.

On the other hand, *rationalists*, following Kant, argue that our apprehension of the world is mediated by our *a priori* linguistic categories, habits of thought, reasoning processes, and theories. The world isn't simply available, and language is the key to our knowledge of it. The issue is thus not whether we need theory, but whether our theoretical frameworks – which, to hark back to Chapter Three, are intimately bound up with ontology, our understanding of the phenomenal nature of the world – are unacknowledged or obvious.

The rationalist position seems to me to be unassailable. As human beings, we appreciate and understand the observable realities of our world only with the aid of frameworks for making sense of the world that are constructed in and out of concrete categories and abstract generalised models (i.e. theories). Our research techniques are part of these frameworks and our theories are cognitive techniques for making sense of the world. Knowing human subjects are unthinkable without these frameworks. This – the rationalist position – is, however, a statement about how humans function: it actually says nothing about the ontological status of the world, whether that be the world of humans or whatever. The world *is* 'there', whether you or I apprehend it or not. Take all the humans away and the universe remains (albeit not quite the same universe in the absence of humans). The properties of things, of the world, do therefore make a difference. There is a reality.

At which point, two crucial epistemological 'buts' must be introduced. First, that there is a reality doesn't mean that it's unproblematically available. This is why we need to distinguish between *reality* and *observable reality*: what we know of the world depends upon our techniques of knowing – whether they be conceptual, mechanical, optical, or whatever – and our embodied senses. In the second place, unlike the universe in general, the *human world* wouldn't exist in the absence of its general human apprehension. In other words, whether *you* or *I* can know the human world isn't the most important epistemological issue. Without a population of self-conscious humans – knowing subjects – apprehending each other and their relationships, there wouldn't be a human world to know. This is why sociological research is *in* or *of* the human world, as well as *into* it.

Affirming the existence and importance of *observable* reality isn't to abandon rationalism. Absolutely the reverse, in fact: everyday realism avoids the naiveties of empiricism in emphasising the difference between reality and observable reality, and in insisting on the necessity of theory *and* research methods in making that observable reality available to us. So this observable reality isn't 'just there' – although it is *there* – it's the product of a process of knowing that's very much part of the human world. This argument recognises that concepts and investigative procedures are, each in equal part, aspects of the cognitive paraphernalia – the framework of knowing – with and through which humans apprehend the world. Theory and method are inseparable, sides of the same coin, both techniques for and of knowing.

What about 'the truth' in all of this? Truth is a big word, but it cannot be evaded if I am to continue talking about 'reality'. Sociological research is about claiming to know something about the observable realities of the human world. It can't be otherwise, and it necessarily implies some sense of truth and falsity. To evoke the shade of Karl Popper, we are most confident in judging something false: any rigorous truth claim is, at least in principle, open to falsification by one deviant instance.[15] In sociological research, however, as in daily life, we conventionally work within greater tolerances than that. We have to.

Allowing for perception via the five senses – particularly hearing (what people say) – and depending upon what it is that we're interested in, in our everyday lives we have a number of overlapping critical procedures that we use to establish the observable realities of 'what's going on'. These are, in alphabetical order:

- comparing events in the present with previous events of which there is knowledge;
- comparing what people say with what people do;
- experimenting: trying stuff out to see how others will respond, or what else will happen;
- mapping: establishing the spatial relationships and characteristics of events and interaction;
- quantifying: counting, measuring, and calculating; and
- timing: establishing recurrence, regularity, sequence, speed, and duration.

Each of these is an approach to the same objective: the identification and establishment of *pattern* in the human world.

Connected to these are the ways in which we defend the plausibility of our claims to know what's going on. The major fault-line here separates *direct* knowledge from *indirect* knowledge: seeing and experiencing for ourselves, or accepting the testimony of others. Whether it is direct or indirect, however, we also have to be able to claim that the knowledge which we are claiming makes *sense*. Direct knowledge is axiomatically more trustworthy than indirect – 'believe half of what you see, and none of what you hear' – but my direct knowledge is, to someone else, necessarily indirect, and *vice versa*. So we need to be able to evaluate the sense of what others tell us, and to argue for the sense of what we claim to know.

Leaving aside linguistic logic – which isn't specific to evidential or truth claims – making sense is a matter of how descriptions and explanations hang together *in context*. Whatever the context, there are always different points of view – participants' and observers' – from which judgements of sense can be made. Even this isn't straightforward, however: there may be no consensus among either participants or observers, and the distinction between being a participant and being an observer isn't always clear. None the less, and allowing for these sources of disagreement, shared membership of the symbolic universes referred to in the previous chapter – i.e. knowledge of the world in common – is significant in establishing some parameters of what makes sense and what doesn't in any particular context.

This brings the discussion back to rationalist epistemology, and the role of existing conventional knowledge in generating and legitimating further knowledge.[16] For truth and knowledge claims to make sense, in the first place, they have to broadly fit into existing legitimate frameworks of knowledge and ways of reasoning. Knowledge that doesn't fit into the normal paradigms is either trashed and vanquished, relegated to its own deviant niche (UFO-ology, for example, or spiritualism) or is required to generate sufficient, and sufficiently accepted, confirming evidence to eventually modify or overturn conventional wisdom. All of these are, at least in part, a matter of politics: gathering support, lobbying, and so on.

This suggests that being able to claim to know 'what's going on', involves knowing two distinct, but connected things: first, what are commonly called *the facts*, and second, *the sense* that they make in context. For example, whether someone said, 'I am a beetle', to someone else is in principle establishable as a fact: either they said it or they didn't. The sense of what they said, what it is taken to mean, is something else again. This crude distinction between facts and their sense can be mapped onto the equally unsophisticated and problematic distinction between methods and theory (problematic, if for no other reason, because technique is necessarily predicated on, and designed with reference to, already existing theorised knowledge).

More problematic again, however, is the recognition that sense-in-context – and it's *always* in context, never absolute – is a kind of fact in its own right. However, this isn't straightforward, either. While it's *possible* to collect evidence, on the basis of which a definitive account of the facts about happenings, or the existence of something or someone, can be robustly defended, we are always likely to encounter different versions of the sense that those facts make. This is because sense is only ever made from a point of view, and every context is likely to include several different points of view. While we may be able to establish – by inquiry, as empirical fact – that all of the points of view present in a situation agree about the sense of something, and on that basis offer a defensible account of that sense, the account can never be *utterly* definitive. Someone may be dissembling or lying, someone may reflect on the matter and change their mind later, there will always be alternative interpretations available, even if they are not represented at any particular time, and so on. Sense changes and is unstable in a way that bare facts are not.

If we acknowledge these reservations, the distinction between the *facts* and their *sense* is revealed as something of a blunt instrument. Blunt or no, however, it has the great virtue of reminding us – whether in common sense or sociological sense – that the facts, fundamental though they are, don't speak for themselves. It's only in bringing together 'the facts' and their 'sense' that the observable realities of the human world can be properly established.

So, what are those observable realities? With what is sociological research concerned? Our empirical data fall into six categories:

- basic numbers, which can include many different kinds of material: demographic or census-style data, bio-medical data about individuals, agricultural data, observational data about attendance at social occasions, and so on;
- what people say: this is essential if we are to understand what the human world means to its members, which explains

why the most important sociological research practice, whether in a survey or an ethnographic field study, is conversation (otherwise known as interviewing);

- everything else that people do (because talk is, after all, something that people do): where it is possible, direct observation is the preferable way to document this;
- explicitly informational and communicative human artefacts are rich sources: everything from texts, to music, to pictures, to the plastic arts;
- other artefacts are also a vital aspect of the constitution and persistence of the human world: this category includes an enormous diversity of things, from buildings to everyday domestic paraphernalia; and
- overlapping with the above, but distinct in its extensive spatiality, its complexity, and its ecological patterns, the human transformation and organisation of the earth and our physical environment is also foundational of the human world, and can be documented.

These kinds of data can all be established as 'bare fact' and endowed with sense in context. They can be seen or heard or touched – even perhaps smelled and tasted – and recorded 'objectively' by machines. Each kind of data can be compared or combined with other data, experimented with (many questions, for example, are actually modest experiments, as are some statistical procedures), mapped, quantified, and timed. Sociologically, each can potentially shed light on any of the others. They can all be approached *individually*, *interactionally* and *institutionally*. Each of the three classificatory orders which combine in my basic interpretive framework for understanding the human world derives analytical substance from all of these observable realities.

Systematic Inquiry

Given these observable realities, how are we as sociologists to explore the human world? How are we to find something out about that world with sufficient confidence to allow us to make defensible statements about it? So far in this chapter, in focusing on everyday realism, my main focus has been on the important epistemological common ground shared by common sense and sociological sense. As I suggested in Chapter Two, however, apart from sociology's explicit, reflexive and elaborated interpretive or *sense-making* frameworks (i.e. theory), an important difference between common sense and sociological sense, which validates the latter, is sociology's access to a broader, deeper and more organised body of knowledge than everyday discourse.

Gathering information of this kind is the job of *systematic inquiry*, using a varied and well-established body of research methods. As different from each other as these investigative procedures are, they share the same fundamental purpose: to gather and collect information about the human world. As sociologists, we can't just depend upon what we think we know, or upon whatever bits and bobs come our way in the course of our daily lives. Most sociological research necessarily relies, to a considerable degree if not totally, on indirect knowledge, and we actively collect and put together – construct isn't too strong a word – the information that we require. The procedures that we adopt to do so are conventionally evaluated according to two different criteria of adequacy, which are roughly equivalent to the crude notions of facticity and sense outlined above.

The first of these, *reliability*, assesses consistency, whether the approach in question will produce broadly comparable results over and over again: perhaps on other occasions, perhaps in other contexts, perhaps in the hands of other researchers. A social survey questionnaire, for example, administered in the same manner, to samples constructed in the same way, at different times, should reliably produce data sets which can sensibly be compared with each other. The facts, in other words, will be of the same kind. There are, however, serious problems with this criterion of reliability. First, as a technical criterion, it isn't sufficient to guarantee the value of research: that data are comparable doesn't mean they will be particularly meaningful. Secondly, in a related point, it misunderstands the generic volatility of the human world: satisfying all of the requirements for reliability will not in itself guarantee comparable results from time A to time B (or from setting to setting). Thirdly, it adds a misleading gloss of science to sociological research. Fourthly, ruthlessly applied it would so limit the portfolio of acceptable sociological research methods that many aspects of the human world would simply be beyond the discipline's limited scope.

Validity, by contrast, refers to whether the concepts, reasoning and interpretive frameworks informing the research, and the data-collecting procedures which are employed, actually mean or 'get at' what they are believed to. Are our questions, for example, understood by our informants in the way that we expect them to be, and thus, do their answers mean what we think they mean? In other words, does what we are doing make sense? Interestingly, the sense that is referred to here is arguably common as well as sociological. The criterion of validity has its own shortcoming in that it isn't ever possible to be *certain* of what things *really* mean to others: ultimately other minds are always a mystery. However, as suggested by both the philosopher Gilbert Ryle[17] and our everyday experience of making reasonable, working judgements about what other people are thinking, this difficulty is probably less awkward and constraining than those posed by the notion of reliability.

Bearing these problems in mind, I want to suggest that the real point of research is to collect information in a manner that is *systematic*. This is one of the most significant differences between sociological sense and common sense. By systematic I mean research that is *sensible, comprehensive, transparent*, and *sceptical*. Together, these four criteria add up to an approach that is properly rigorous. If we claim to know something, we have to be able to say why we are making that claim. These four criteria allow us to explain to others the basis on which we are making whatever truth claims we are offering. They allow us to claim a defensible authority for our findings and conclusions. Other people – whether sociologists or not – have to be able to look at our work and see for themselves what its strengths and weaknesses are. This is an aspect of Bauman's 'responsible speech':[18] the responsibility in question here is our duty to be able to defend the authority and plausibility of whatever we have to say.

Looking at each of these criteria in turn, what is required for research to be *sensible*? It simply means that any piece of research should gather information which is useful, bearing in mind the researcher's objectives. For example:

- we should try to collect material that is relevant (bearing in mind that what's relevant is often most obvious with the benefit of hindsight);
- we should try to make sure that our questions are valid, that they 'get at' what we think they do; and
- we should try to ensure that our questions are intelligible, given the contexts in which they're going to be asked.

In line with the rationalist epistemology which informs this discussion, these mundane suggestions presuppose that one knows quite a bit about the context or topic in question before beginning the research: this is obviously also an argument for the value of piloting research. Knowing quite a bit in advance can be a problem in its own right, however, because this can sometimes lead to things being taken for granted, or overlooked. So 'being sensible' is equally an argument for perpetual reflexivity, and the ongoing review and revision of what one is doing so that it makes the best sense in context. What 'being sensible' doesn't mean, however, is there is always one best way to do things.

By *comprehensive*, second, I mean the attempt to cover properly the many aspects of the situation or issue that we are looking at. Since the human world is complex, much will depend here on the resources that are available. Much will depend upon which aspects of the situation are thought to be important or relevant, which comes back to being sensible, and relates to a range of factors. Our theoretical presuppositions, for example, influence what's included within the scope of any particular piece of research, as do less elevated factors such as the interests and demands of our paymasters, and the political or institutional climate. Objectivity is clearly at stake here: in principle, a socio-logical stance requires that attention should be paid to all the voices that are present in whatever situation is under investiga-tion, no matter what they're saying, or how awkward it is.

This is an indefensibly idealistic proposition, however. Much will depend upon what's possible in context. Although what is perhaps most surprising is the relative ease with which researchers usually arrange access, it is never automatic and is constrained by considerations of privacy, by power, and by the limits of persuasion: this is one reason – although only one – why sociology underperforms with respect to research on the power-ful and élites. They are simply better placed to say no.[19] Finally, comprehensiveness can refer to information sources or to the questions asked. All other things being equal, however, the one certain thing is that no research can look at absolutely everything. All research is partial and limited, and in every project there are necessary decisions to be made about how comprehensive its scope can be. The aspiration, however, remains important.

Transparency, third, is generally considered to be part of what's meant by reliability. It means that whatever we do when we're gathering information should be open to inspection by others in as much detail as possible. Everybody else should be able to know as much as we can tell them about what we are doing. While considerations of confidentiality and privacy which seem to me insuperable – and as an ethnographer I would, perhaps, say this, wouldn't I? – mean that I can't go all the way with John Goldthorpe, for example, in advocating strin-gent standards of inspectable transparency across the board,[20] perhaps even with respect to original field notes, transparency should apply in some degree to all research. It has two main aspects:

- full explanation to the subjects and/or facilitators of the research, which means, in the first place, opening up and justifying the process while it is ongoing; and

- full explanation to the various audiences for the research – which, of course, includes its subjects or facilitators – which means subsequently justifying findings and conclusions.

Transparency thus means explaining in detail the process of the actual data-gathering, and its implications for the kind and amount of material collected. It means presenting as much as possible of the data on which the conclusions of the research are based, in such a way that the relationship between data, arguments and conclusions can be seen. If relevant, transparency means explaining the workings of any statistical or similar techniques that are used. In principle, it means allowing legitimately interested parties access to one's data, where possible (and to repeat, the only acceptable restrictions on access to primary data that I can think of derive from ethical criteria of confidentiality and privacy). It should also mean writing in a style and language that are as clear and straightforward as possible: transparency extends to all aspects of the research process, from start to finish.

Finally, what about *scepticism*? One of the practical attitudes which this suggests is a reluctance to accept the first answer that we get, or arrive at. It's our sociological responsibility to go beyond common sense, although this doesn't mean, either, that we should imagine that we always know best, or that we should neglect the knowledgeability of the people we are researching. Scepticism means that we should always look for corroboration, and that we should accept nothing without evidence. It means that we should seek evidence from as many different sources as possible (which brings us back to comprehensiveness). And – just to complicate matters – it also means that we should bear in mind that even if evidence for something comes from a number of directions, that doesn't necessarily mean that it's accurate. In this sense, the sceptical attitude that we should cultivate as researchers is nothing more than a self-conscious and more thoroughgoing version of the attitude that it's sensible to adopt in everyday life.

We should also, of course, be perpetually mildly sceptical about ourselves and our research practices. While this is not a call for iconoclasm or total relativism, we should be at least a little wary of the orthodoxies and taken-for-granted bodies of knowledge that have accrued and accreted within sociology, as in any discipline. Scepticism also means that we should, on principle, be critical of other social science accounts of the same phenomenon that we are researching (if only because we'll never be able to learn from them otherwise). Conventional wisdom is only ever that – conventional – and scepticism is one of the most important guarantors of proper sociological reflexivity and the necessary openness that underwrites whatever truth claims we *can* make.

There are other kinds of conventional wisdom too, particularly for an enterprise which is necessarily a part of the phenomenon that it studies. While scepticism obviously implies a refusal to allow ourselves to become the pliant providers of politically palatable evidence in support of this or that policy (*especially* when we agree with it), the intellectual costs of insisting that everything we do should be 'useful' are less obvious, but none the less real. Someone, somewhere, has to define usefulness, after all: it isn't simply a given. C. Wright Mills had a vision in this respect of sociologists becoming no more than 'administrative technicians' in the service of practicality (whether liberal or illiberal).[21] This remains a fate worth avoiding.

So there it is: systematic sociological inquiry should be sensible, comprehensive, transparent and critical. These are not, however, purely technical or epistemological matters to do with undertaking the best possible or most accurate research. Ethical issues are at stake as well, to hark back again to Bauman's notion of 'responsible speech'. The responsibility that we have to make our research as true as we possibly can, is also a *duty* which we owe to our research subjects, to the rest of sociology and the academy, and – whether they always recognise it or not – to our direct and indirect funders. A further responsibility that we owe to the same constituencies is to make what we do as transparent and non-mysterious as possible. Finally, we have a responsibility to maintain an independent critical position in what we do, and to be able to support that position with defensible evidence.

Necessarily, and from whatever perspective it is done, socio-logical research – *in* the human world as well as *into* it – cannot be anything other than an ethically sensitive activity.

At which point it is appropriate to look again at *objectivity*. Along with theory and systematic inquiry, objectivity is the third leg of the sociological stool, the other thing that distinguishes what we do from common sense. It should be the general stance that we adopt towards the human world. Given my argument that the human world is an observable reality – or, to be perhaps more precise, is composed of observable realities – only the best, and the most honest, observations are good enough. As I have already argued, this doesn't mean that we can make sense of the world of humans without pre-existing conceptual frameworks for doing so. Nor does it mean that our methods are innocent, neutral techniques.

What objectivity *does* mean is that we must stand as far back as possible from whatever it is that we are interested in, so that we can have the clearest, most comprehensive view possible. It means endeavouring, all the time, to prevent our politics and values getting in the way of discovering as much as we can, as honestly as we can, and as systematically as we can. This is a matter of sensible, comprehensive, transparent, and sceptical research – of permanent reflexivity – and it suggests that theory, systematic inquiry, and objectivity are, in research practice, difficult to disentangle. It doesn't mean, however, that we should have no interest in what we find out, or that we shouldn't *care*: sociological research is, necessarily, *in* the human world as well as *about* it.

Choosing Methods

From what I've said so far it should be clear that I'm not going to advocate the superiority or otherwise of particular sociological research approaches. Reviewing the wide range of methods and approaches that sociologists use to collect and construct data – social surveys, the analysis of secondary data sets, archival and documentary studies, case-studies, the collection of life histories, in-depth interviewing, ethnographic participant observation, and this doesn't begin to exhaust the possibilities – the only sensible conclusion that I can come to is that they each do *some* things better, or just *rather*, than other things. Choice in this respect is a matter of horses for courses, and the complexity of the human world means that the most successful research is often a matter of combining approaches and methods.

This is not an attempt to please everyone – it won't – nor is it well-meaning liberal tolerance. It's simply the only conclusion that I can come to on the basis of a research career which has, at one time or another, involved all of the above approaches to data collection. A healthy, pluralist promiscuity of method seems to me the only stance to adopt if one's curiosity about the human world is not to be constrained by methodological prejudice or inertia. Allowing that to happen would be another way to put the cart before the horse.

The longest-running, best known, and possibly most irritating, example of this kind of non-problem is the well-worn debate about the respective value of quantitative and qualitative research methods. Put bluntly, the difference between the two is the difference between two questions:

- How many people do or say something [*quantity*]? and,
- What does that something mean to the people who are doing it [*quality*]?

This is, of course, broadly analogous with the distinction between behaviour (*society*) and meaning (*culture*) that I discussed in Chapter Three. As with that distinction, the contrast between the quantitative and the qualitative is not as clear-cut or definite as it appears to be from the manner in which some sociologists discuss it.

Drawing here on the increasingly widely accepted arguments of non-sectarian methodologists such as Alan Bryman,[22] this issue can be approached in a number of ways. For example, before counting can be a sensible activity, one must know *what* to count, and *which* questions to ask in order to find out about whatever it is that one wants to count. Each of these depends upon knowing and understanding the *meaning* of things. Coming from the other direction, the meaning of phenomena in the human world is heavily bound up with *number*. For example, for two people to remove all of their clothes on a crowded beach is one thing. Several hundred people stripping off on a crowded beach suggests something else, however, while everybody nude on a crowded beach is an altogether different situation. The situations in each case have different meanings and quantity is at the heart of that qualitative difference.

Each approach, the quantitative and the qualitative, is attempting to find out what's going on in the human world. That they are doing so by asking rather different questions – and different questions are obviously appropriate for different projects – doesn't mean that number and meaning are in any sense opposites: the quantitative and the qualitative are complementary rather than contradictory. That this argument won't convince the die-hards in either camp is a depressing reflection on the depth and pathos of individual investment in such matters, but it still cannot be reiterated too often.

This isn't just a matter of the distinction between culture/meaning and society/behaviour, however. Within the quantitative/qualitative dualism another distinction – between the individual and the collective – is also being played out. One conventional view in this respect is that quantitative research collects aggregate data about atomistic *individuals*, their attributes, behaviour, and attitudes, whereas qualitative research most typically collects information about the *relationships* and interaction between people, and about shared meanings.[23] The sub-text here is generally something along the lines of: 'relationships good, individuals bad'.

There is, thank goodness, more to be said about the issue than this. Any research that involves collecting data in the field – whether it be a huge doorstep survey, or an intimate long-term ethnography – is dependent on collecting primary data from and about individuals. It cannot be otherwise, given that individuals are the most visible and significant of the observable realities of the human world. Elsewhere I have coined the expression 'pragmatic individualism' to characterise both the common-sense attitude to the human world, and the everyday realism without which sociological research would be impossible.[24] The practicalities of understanding the human world are necessarily founded on the existence of individuals: there isn't really anywhere else that one can begin. Even texts have their authors and artefacts their makers.

Qualitative research, what's more, is typically more interested in the depths of individuality and its distinctiveness than quantitative research. That qualitative research can bring to the sociological study of collectivity a sense of fully-rounded, three-dimensional, living-in-the-world, decision-making, individual humans is, indeed, one of its great strengths. Quantitative research, on the other hand, is concerned, perhaps much more than anything else, with the identification and exploration of pattern – and pattern is as definitively non-individual as it is possible to imagine – in bodies of data about pluralities of humans.

To say that quantitative research focuses on individuals, while qualitative research deals with the collective, is therefore a simplification, at best. At worst, it's completely misleading. There are, none the less, significant differences in these respects between the two approaches. Analytically, each broad school of sociological research brings the individual and the collective together in different ways. Quantitative research, to return to the point made above, is capable of aggregating data about individuals and revealing established patterns in the human world in a way that qualitative research simply can't. Those patterns are among the clearest ways in which the individual, the interactional and the institutional orders reveal themselves to be, as I suggested in Chapter Four, an analytical trinity, based on and in the physical space occupied by real, embodied individuals.

If they are nothing else, these patterns are a definitive and essential aspect of the more-than-the-sum-of-the-parts with which this book is centrally concerned. Furthermore, as Anthony Giddens among others has pointed out, the sociological elucidation of pattern has become part and parcel of the governance and organisation of the modern human world: *in* that world as well as *about* it.[25] Amid the volume, density, distance, and complexity of modernity, those patterns contribute to the reflexive constitution of a sense that there is something-more-than-the-sum-of-the-parts. That people know about the collective patterns of their lives is, at least in part, and whether directly or indirectly, a consequence of sociological research. Many of those patterns are aspects of the observable reality of the human world which, without systematic inquiry, would not otherwise be visible in everyday common sense. Quantitative research thus permits us to perceive the contours of the human world, as well as the very obvious individual humans who live in it, who produce and reproduce it, who *are* it.

If, to take liberties with Peter Berger's original words,[26] quantitative research is, therefore, particularly good at looking at 'humans in the human world', qualitative research is adept at infiltrating and interpreting 'the human world in humans'. There are at least three, overlapping, senses in which this is so. In the first, qualitative research can offer detailed insights into the workings of everyday life, characterised as it is by messy and complex relationships between the collective or shared and the individual, between what it is believed people ought to do and what they actually do, between the conflicting demands of obligations to others, individual decision-making, and compulsion. Secondly, the powerful imperatives of symbolism, which are vital if we are to understand how individuality and collectivity reciprocally inform and imply each other without any need for overweaning consensus, are best understood and their workings best explained qualitatively. Finally, the reality and solidity of institutions, and their constraining and enabling properties for individuals, can be understood at least as well through ethnographic observation from within, as through the documentation of statistical pattern from without. And the view in each case is different.

Of course, neither qualitative nor quantitative sociology is sufficient if we are to understand better the human world, and the relationships between individuality and collectivity in and through which it is constituted and reconstituted daily. Without systematic evidence of pattern, we simply wouldn't know enough about the consequences, intended or unintended, of individual lives, or their persistence and change; we certainly couldn't have sufficient understanding of the frameworks of constraint and enablement within which individuals' lives are lived. On the other hand, without complex and nuanced understandings of why and – no less important – *how* people do whatever they do in everyday life, our interpretation of quantitative pattern would be shallow at best, and unreal at worst. Where else should the assumptions upon which complex statistical modelling depends, come from? From the common sense of the modellers? From the simplifying – but over-simple – assumptions of rational-choice theorists? Heaven forbid, because neither seems to hold much promise. Furthermore, institutions, the study of which is right at the heart of sociological knowledge of the human world, are utterly impossible to understand adequately without both quantitative and qualitative insight into their observable realities.

It's implicit in what's been said so far that social change, the other key sociological theme, is also approached differently by quantitative and qualitative sociology. Qualitative research reveals complex processes in which change is the product of many factors and often unintended, but this research is hampered by its shortcomings with respect to chronological depth. Quantitative research, on the other hand, can comfortably handle long-term data sets, but is necessarily somewhat superficial. As in so much else, the challenge lies in recognising the complementarity of the two approaches, and devising successful strategies for incorporating into practical empirical research the gains offered by each.

In this chapter, I have suggested that the epistemological assumptions of sociology overlap to a considerable degree with those of common sense. Without everyday realism, systematic sociological inquiry is pretty much unthinkable. We assume that there is an observable reality – the human world – made up of people and things, what people say and do and make, and the physical environment that they shape. Trying to understand 'what's going on' in the human world involves establishing the facts, and making sense of them. The distinctiveness of sociological sense comes from the systematic procedures of inquiry that sociologists use to establish the facts, from our explicit and extensive frameworks for making sense of them, and from the stance that we adopt towards them. Research, theory, and objectivity: in sociological practice these are utterly implicated in each other.

The physical environment is not, however, simply an inert 'something' that is 'out there' to be shaped by humans. The wider world and universe – stretching as far away into the distance as it is possible to imagine, and then beyond – affects to a greater or lesser degree, and in every imaginable sense, the human world. The next chapter will present a preliminary account of how we might understand the relationships between humans and that natural world.

Six

The Human World and the Natural World

The disciplines which I have brought together under the umbrella of 'generic sociology' are all firmly rooted in the common-sensical point of view that a difference of kind separates humans from the rest of the world, and 'culture' from 'nature'. This anthropocentric cosmology has its deepest direct roots in a Judaeo-Christian theology which imagines human beings as created in the image of God and granted dominion over the rest of creation. Within sociology, the assumption of the separation of humanity and nature is sufficiently consensual to be almost invisible – it's the ontological and moral air that most of us breathe – and all the more powerful for that.

For various pressing reasons it is increasingly an assumption that won't do. The environmental peril into which we have delivered ourselves suggests that we are an integral part of the eco-sphere, not invulnerable to its condition. New biological science has implications for our understanding of the nature and sources of human competences and of the contribution of our organic embodiment to who and what humans are. Finally, the analytical constraints under which we labour as sociologists because of our assumptions about humanity's place in the natural world are becoming increasingly obvious. In this chapter I want to lay some foundations for the discussions that we need to have if we are to move towards a more integrated sociological understanding of the relationship between the human world and the natural world. Although this may also change our understanding of the natural world, it is our better understanding of the human world which is primarily at stake.

Sociology and Biology

So, orthodox sociological ontology is rooted in an axiomatic human–centred cosmology which understands humans and animals as of fundamentally different *kinds*. Within this perspective, the relationship between humans and their natural environments is oppositional (if not actually adversarial), exploitative, and hierarchical. Humans manipulate and rule nature, we are not part of it.[1] Through the application of our formidable intellects, the mobilisation of our capacity for collective organisation, and the transformative powers of our technologies, we have gradually loosened the shackles that for many millennia bound us to the earth's seasonal cycles and climate zones and to our physiological limitations as an organism. This anthropocentric cosmology is recognisably the universe of expansionist modernity and progress: a universe that is acted upon, under human sway, increasingly rendered manageable and predictable. Within sociology this perspective has typically allowed the natural world to be bracketed off, as external to what we're interested in. Many of us who support green politics and environmentalism might be dismayed and perplexed by the unexamined assumptions of our sociology in this respect.

These deeply buried fundamentals inform a number of more explicit articles of sociological faith. Perhaps most important is the belief that biology and physiology have little or no role to play in explaining the 'social' or 'cultural' phenomena which interest sociologists. Here, ancient and axiomatic anthropomorphism is in harmony with relatively new social movements such as feminism which have struck a loud chord within post-1960s sociology. Whether it be gender inequality or disability – for example – the 'problem' and the 'differences' are, in as much as sociologists are interested in them, understood to be socially constructed.[2] To suggest otherwise is indecent. The notion of human nature also appears to be sociologically heretical. Instead of exploring the similarities which constitute humanity as a species, the apparently limitless plasticity of human behaviour and cultural difference is celebrated, a doctrine which has been further elaborated and promulgated under the banner of postmodernism.[3] Finally, while technology or organisational features may be evoked as explanations of this or that, to mention the environment as an influence on human behaviour is likely to provoke accusations of determinism. As a consequence the contemporary sociology of the environment turns out to be largely the sociology of environmental*ism* and perceived risk.[4]

In all of these respects, the vast majority of sociologists are radical social constructionists. However, the self-imposed analytical constraints on sociology mentioned above have not gone unnoticed, and interesting recent exceptions to this general rule, each in their different way, include Margaret Archer, Michael Carrithers, Abram de Swaan, Adam Kuper, W. G. Runciman, and Bryan Turner and Chris Rojek,[5] a list which might suggest that an interesting space may at last be opening up for the discussion of alternative perspectives. For the moment, however, biology and nature remain almost dirty words within sociology.

This sociological catechism, summarised as baldly as I have just done, overlooks much of the subtlety of generations of scholarship across the range of endeavours that I have characterised as generic sociology. What's more, to repeat an earlier point, it's important to recognise that many – probably most – sociologists would explain themselves by insisting that all they are actually doing is bracketing off biology and the 'natural' as a simplifying assumption for the focused purposes of sociological inquiry. This response is inadequate, however. Setting to one side something that makes a difference to how we understand the world of humans cannot possibly be helpful.

The sociological orthodoxy can't be rejected out of hand, however. The environment *has* been brought under human dominion to an extent that would have seemed unimaginable even a couple of hundred years ago.[6] Human behaviour *is* extraordinarily open-ended and flexible. It *is* undoubtedly the case that much – perhaps most – of the disadvantage experienced by women or people with disabilities, for example, has got nothing to do with biology and physiology. In other words, social constructionism takes us a very long way towards understanding the human world. It is *the* necessary foundation of sociology: nothing is more fundamental. What's more, given the dreadful ways in which ideas about human biology have figured – and continue to figure – in the oppression of women and the tyranny of male domination, in slavery, in genocide, in the forced sterilisation and medical terrorisation of the 'unfit', and in a variety of coercive 'therapies', it is extraordinarily important that we resist the biological determinism that informs much common sense and science.

As sociologists, we will not do that most effectively, however, if we turn our backs on biology and nature, as if they had nothing to do with us. In this chapter, therefore, I want to develop further two suggestions that were made in earlier chapters:

- first, that the human world and the natural world are systematically implicated in each other, not separated by a difference of kind; and
- second, that my approach to making sense of the human world allows for a multi-directional or ecological approach to the relationships between that world and the natural world.

I am in fact going to argue that the human world is best understood as part of the 'natural world'. This is a model the application of which is given further impetus if we recognise that the 'natural world' is every bit a human construction.[7] It's a notion that only makes sense from the point of view of, and in counterpoise to, the human world. There almost certainly isn't a 'natural world' *as such* for any other species.

The Natural World

The last paragraph raises an issue of terminology (and perhaps something more basic). The expression 'the natural world' has its shortcomings: most problematically it suggests the possibility that the human world might be somehow non-natural. This is very far from my intention. Furthermore, the 'natural world' might also be taken to imply a more definite and bounded reality than I have in mind. I have, therefore, considered alternatives. Of 'the non-reflexive world', 'the non-human world', 'the physical world', 'the biological world', 'the ecological world', and 'the environmental world', none is any better, and some muddy the waters even further. Variations on the theme of 'the universe' or 'the cosmos', on the other hand, are too enormous and sublime for what I have in mind: when viable non-umbilical space travel becomes an option, we can reconsider the matter, but at least for the moment I want to keep my feet on the planet. 'The natural world' allows me at least to do that, and is relatively simple.

'The natural world' it's going to be then, a world which includes the human world. In principle, it also includes an incalculable multitude of spatially-overlapping, and in evolutionary terms symbiotic, sensory-perceptual and experiential worlds: everything, perhaps, from 'the blue whale world', to whatever the worlds of bacteria or viruses might be. The human world is only one of these and in no sense the most evolved or important (except to us). At a different level of abstraction, the human world itself is also, of course, a mosaic of overlapping collective and individual experiential worlds. Sociology, in this sense, is but one of a range of human views *of* and *from* (or *in*) the human world.

Human Nature, Human Needs

Writing not long after the rival first-draft maps of the human genome were finally published,[8] *human nature* is an obvious place to begin unpacking some of the connections between the natural world and the human world. To judge from the spin put on their findings by both of the research teams concerned, these turn out, interestingly enough, to be relevant here. The relatively small number of genes that we now know humans to possess – small in comparison with fruit flies or certain worms, for example – indicates that most of the complexities of human behaviour are unlikely to be specifically genetically programmed. The search for the 'gay gene', for example, has almost certainly been futile.

Whether that's good or bad news, I'll leave the reader to decide, but it does suggest some observations about human nature. Looking around at what we know about the range of human behaviour, what do we humans appear to have in common as a species (which isn't the same as asking what's *peculiar* to humans)? In no order of priority, the following are among the most obvious answers to the question:

- adaptability and the preparedness to explore and exploit a huge diversity of physical environments;
- sociality, which includes competition as well as co-operation;
- organisation into groups that differentiate themselves from other groups;
- abiding bonds between kin, particularly parents and children;
- a long phase of dependency and necessary socialisation during early life;
- opposable thumbs, giving the ability to produce complex artefacts;
- insatiable curiosity about ourselves and the world;
- non-utilitarian playfulness;
- imagination and the ability to transcend the observable realities of the visible world;
- detailed and extensive memories;
- an enormously effective intelligence, combining life-long learning with the ability to rationalise, calculate and plan;
- complex, symbol-based communication systems;
- free will, the capacity to choose among alternatives;
- sexual enthusiasm, which, with its range of orientations and preferences, is not confined to procreation;
- a wide range of emotions, from euphoria to depression; and
- individual reflexivity, the capacity to take the part of the other, to see and think about ourselves as others do.

This list isn't even close to being a last word on the subject, but it suffices to make my point. *All* of the above can be found in *all* human groups, and taken together they point to three related conclusions:

- first, it's human nature to be flexible and behaviourally open: plasticity, although it isn't infinite, seems to be definitive of humanity, our instincts don't seem to give us much guidance;
- second, it's human nature to do the range of things that we conventionally gloss as 'culture': without communication, learning and invention we would be quite different creatures (and we'd never have got where we are today); and
- third, individuality and collectivity are both natural and, far from being irreconcilable, are complementary.

I am not sure that we really needed the results of the Human Genome Project – welcome as they are – to tell us that humans *in their very natures* are adaptable, open, sociable, cultural beings.[9] How could it be otherwise? What would it mean to be as adaptively successful – in the 'red in tooth and claw' sense – as humans have been as a species, in all manner of environments, if we were not somehow doing 'what comes naturally'? This is how we have evolved: as the brightest, most all-purpose, most adaptable – to the cost of most other species, irresistible – primate. This is our genetic species-being.

It is also our predicament. The human condition is fundamentally ambiguous. Our evolutionary fate is not only to dominate, but also to realise that we are doing so, and to understand, as individuals, that our time on the planet is finite. The knowledge of our own death, and the realisation of time in past and future tenses, informs much of what we call 'culture' and imbues all aspects of everyday life. This too must be added to whatever it is that we think of as 'human nature'.

Looking at our natural capacities and our existential condition isn't the only way to approach human nature, however. What, for example, are our species-specific *needs*? Once again, I doubt that we need a complex knowledge of genetics to think about this. There is an old and extensive philosophical literature about human needs:[10] it is almost as if we are happier talking about our needs than our nature, despite the obvious interdependence of these concepts. There is, for example, a set of assumptions about human needs – about what it might mean to be a fully-realised human being – to be found in Marx.[11] Psychoanalysis, rooted as it is, among other things, in Freud's ideas about the self-preservational and sexual drives, clearly assumes the existence of needs.[12] Subsequently, in the 1940s Abraham Maslow famously articulated a hierarchical priority of needs, from the most basic, the purely organic, to the most luxurious, the need for self-actualisation.[13] Politics concerns needs, too. The opening lines of the American Constitution refer to 'liberty and the pursuit of happiness', and any defence of human *rights* necessarily depends on some model of human *needs*. Welfare state social democracy is a statement about what humans are thought to need, for example, as are current policy debates within the European Union about the 'quality of life'.[14]

From a broadly sociological perspective, the contribution of Len Doyal and Ian Gough to our thinking about these matters is fundamental. In addition to problematising the tricky distinction between *needs* and *wants*, they argue that the basic human needs of physical health and autonomy are dependent for their actualisation on a set of more specific intermediate needs, such as food and water, housing, non-hazardous environments, security in childhood, and education.[15] Abram de Swaan, approaching the same issues, identifies the human needs of food, shelter, protection, affection, knowledge, and direction, and highlights socialisation as the process which brings to fruition whatever inborn capacities humans have.[16] In broad outline, Doyal and Gough and de Swaan are offering very similar models of human needs. On the one hand, there's what we need for physical survival, on the other what we need to maintain the distinctiveness of our humanity, with neither body nor soul having priority. Both are dependent for their satisfaction on relationships with other humans.

How human needs are satisfied confronts us with the openness of human nature. In terms of diet, humans are pretty much omnivorous. Shelters can be constructed from stone or ice, wood or sod, paper or skin, metal or plastic. We protect ourselves with technology and collective organisation in all of their diversity, and in combination with each other. Affection can flow between kin, friends, sexual partners, and strangers. Knowledge is potentially as infinite as the natural world itself, and its sources are many and remain important all the way through life. Finally, direction – control and guidance – which depends on internalisation, coercion, rational calculation, and the channelling effects of the infrastructure of the human world, is for humans the vital precondition of individual autonomy and self-realisation.

Human Bodies

The post-Holocaust realisation of where 'race' and eugenics lead, and the ways in which physiology can be used to legitimate gender conservatism, have made sociologists understandably reluctant to admit biology into discussions of such matters. This cannot, however, continue indefinitely. If, for example, we want to reach a non-determinist understanding of human identification in all its aspects – an explanation that preserves our sociological sense that the human world is a human construction – then we can only do so by trying to understand how human physiology *does* fit into the picture. We cannot just define it away as irrelevant or beyond the scope of sociology, nor can we simply confine our attention to the social construction of embodiment.[17] There is more to the embodiment of humanity than that.

Embodiment makes a particularly clear contribution to identification with respect to *difference*. Perhaps the most obvious sense in which this matters is in routine individual difference: facial features, height, weight, shape, hair and eye colour, complexion, smell. Individual physical variety is a complex interplay between genetic endowment – whether hereditary or the result of damage or mutation – environmental factors, and deliberate modification. So far, so good, and so mundane. Any busy street in any town is a cavalcade of individual diversity: it is the human norm.

Matters change, generally for the worse, when individual differences become the building blocks of collective categorisation.

Look at 'race', for example. Over evolutionary time, human populations have developed which, as a consequence of environmentally adaptive selection and its reproductive transmission, are characterised, in the context of a wide range of other variations, by particular patterns of individual embodiment. Biologically, however, these are still *individual* characteristics and *individual* variations, which are only transmitted or modified generationally as a result of *individuals* mating. Within all human populations diversity remains the norm, and what remains strikingly obvious is the basic similarity of all humans with each other. In other words, there are no 'races'. There are merely very complex, overlapping and ever-changing patterns of visible and invisible *individual* genetic variety.[18]

Unfortunately, this isn't obvious to everyone. Within relatively recent historical time, in a human world that is organised into groups which distinguish themselves from each other, the mundane visibility of certain, and only certain, physical differences has been reconstructed into notions of 'racial' difference which impose on patterns of unremarkable individual variation hierarchies of collective worth and essence, hierarchies which can be unforgiving in their inflexibility and which have inspired and legitimated dispossession, slavery, and genocide. In Europe and East Asia, in particular, these ideas developed, unsurprisingly enough, in the context of expansionist imperialism.[19] In extreme versions, 'racial' categorisations have fractured and denied unitary human-ness itself, in a triumph of social construction over the observable realities of everyday life *and* science.[20]

In the case of 'physical disability', embodiment and identification come together differently. A more modern notion than 'race', one hundred and fifty years ago 'the disabled' didn't exist as a category. Instead, there were 'cripples', 'the infirm', 'the deaf', 'the blind', 'the mute', 'the deformed', and so on. Today, by contrast, there is a Disability Movement. The array of individual differences which that movement welcomes is as staggering as the diversity of their causes: ageing, genetic endowment, illness, accident, environmental hazard, and deliberate violence. And yet, despite this panorama of diversity – to recognise which is to respect the observable realities of impairment, not to ignore them – we find ourselves faced with a powerful unitary category: 'people with physical disabilities'.[21]

'People with physical disabilities' are individuals who are classified, by those who claim expert knowledge, as unable by virtue of their embodiment to participate in everyday life as competently as 'the able-bodied'. The modern category of 'disability' is, to follow the arguments of authors such as Michael Oliver and Deborah Stone,[22] in large part a bureaucratic and political construction of the capitalist state. In a system in which there isn't enough productive activity for everyone, 'disability' excuses a slice of the population from the labour force – on grounds which don't threaten the work ethic – and facilitates their administration within the welfare system. There's more to it than that, of course: impairment *is* a reality, being categorised as 'disabled' can be an escape route from the worst excesses of a harsh life, and a kernel of compassion, at least, can be discerned in the whole business. None the less, the creation of 'the disabled' has been another victory for homogenising social construction over the observable realities of individual human difference.

These are two cases in which embodied individual diversity – only some of which is unambiguously, unconstructedly 'natural' – has been categorised into powerful imaginings of collective sameness. In the case of 'race', the reality of that diversity is, in the absence of categorisation, skin-deep, absurdly superficial. The physical impairments that provide the category of 'disability' with its logic, while they are anything but absurd, vary greatly in their causes and consequences.

If 'race' and 'disability' are imaginings constructed in and out of the lumpen categorisation of individual differences, gender, the other embodied difference that I want to look at, is somewhat different. There are non-constructed, natural differences in the embodiment of female and male humans which no amount of mating and mingling can modify. Gender is based on a *general* difference of embodied *type*. Men and women differ in the following organically embodied ways, which have nothing to do with social construction:

- women can bear and breast-feed babies;
- women's life-times and everyday lives are temporally structured by fertility: menarche, menstruation, and menopause;
- men and women are dimorphic: they differ markedly in their skeletal structure, in the distribution and amount of muscle and body fat, men are on average taller, heavier, and stronger than women;[23]
- men and women function differently sexually: men are constrained with respect to performance – the hydraulics of erection – and frequency of orgasm, in ways that women are not (which is not to suggest that women experience no sexual constraints, or to pass any judgement on the multiplicity of the female orgasm);
- women can, at least in principle, be absolutely certain of the maternity of their children – birth is obvious and definite – whereas until very recently men could not be certain of paternity.

These are, I hope, relatively uncontroversial facts about the biological differences between male and female bodies, observable realities in the sense that was discussed in the previous chapter. They can be placed in further necessary context by three other observations:

- almost uniquely among mammals, women are physically sexually receptive all year round;[24]
- the long-term dependence of infants on women for their basic survival needs has only very recently begun to change with the development of alternatives to breast milk; and
- as far as we know, the pattern of relations between men and women has universally featured gendered spatial arrangements and divisions of labour, and differential socialisation.

Remembering the arguments of Chapter Five, what matters is the sense that we make of these facts: they do not speak for themselves. The sense we make depends, in the first place, on what we are trying to understand. Perhaps the most obvious puzzle is, why patriarchy? Why do men dominate women? In this context, the first thing to note is that none of the facts I have presented might be thought to *determine* that women should be oppressed or dominated by men. That, in other words, is *not* natural: in the two linked interpretations that shackle our thinking about what's natural or not, male domination is neither *inevitable* nor *alright* (or right).

These facts about the natural, embodied differences between men and women do, however, suggest the beginnings of a plausible understanding of how and why male domination is ubiquitous in the human world and human history. The core of that understanding has several components, once again in no order of priority:

- men have, until very recently, had no way of identifying their offspring with certainty, and in a kin-oriented human world that mattered;
- for men, sexual intercourse can be insecure and vulnerable (pygmy chimpanzees may be able to do it all day and every day, but human males can't);
- men often appear to think that women are permanently available for sexual activity (to say which says nothing about what women might want or feel or do); and
- for millennia, men and women have to some considerable extent inhabited separate spheres of the human world, reproductively, temporally, spatially, and productively.

At this point, it might be objected that this is largely a male perspective on sex differences. Yes it is, and that shouldn't be an objection. Since it's the behaviour of men – and let's remember that the argument doesn't depend on this being the behaviour of *all* men – that's largely been the problem, it seems to be a reasonable and sensible direction from which to begin making sense of the matter. It suggests that men are, or have been:

- open to feelings of sexual inadequacy;
- uncertain about the paternity of their children; and
- unable to satisfy directly some of their offsprings' long-term basic human needs.

Furthermore, the meanings of these problems were and are worked out in contexts in which men and women spent and spend a great deal of their adult time in same-sex company.

On the one hand there is insecurity, on the other *de facto* exclusion. Men's responses have not been determined in any sense – so this can't be interpreted as an apologia – but their greater strength and weight have allowed them to assert at least a semblance of control over women's sexuality and fertility through physical force or its threat (although men and women have always known that the relations between them are more complicated than that). Since the openness of our nature allows humans to be aggressive as well as co-operative, to pursue individual and collective advantage as well as to deny it, there was and is no natural behavioural block to men doing so. Men may have oppressed women *in response* to perceived difficulties that were naturally part of the biology of embodiment, but they have done so because they *could*. Not because they *had* to. Given the centrality of women to reproduction and socialisation – to human life – men flexed their greater muscles. Even relative equality of weight and strength between the sexes might have made all the difference. It is surely no coincidence that feminism began and has prospered when and where the public use of violence has been limited and placed, at least nominally, under the monopoly of the modern state.

This, of course, is a simplification, necessarily so since it's the tentative outline of an interpretation, painted with a very broad brush. It's incomplete: there are many details of the argument which require development.[25] It's also speculative, equally necessarily. Although we know more of the facts than Friedrich

Engels did in *The Origin of the Family, Private Property and the State*,[26] the archaeological, historical, and ethnographic records are far from complete, and will remain so. However, this is a socio-logical interpretation that adds something to present discussions – within 'corporeal feminism' for example[27] – by permitting into the argument a range of biological facts wider than those pertaining to reproduction, and about men as well as women.

To return to the discussion of change in Chapter Four, this isn't a matter of predictive law-like certainty. The human world doesn't work like that. The openness of human nature, the real-ity of enormous individual human variation, and the diversity of environments in which humans make a living, combine to insist that there is great variation in how the biology of *sexual* differ-ence becomes the organisation of *gender*, between and within human groups. Nor does my argument suggest that women have simply been passive victims, incapable of making their own contributions to the situation. In all of these respects, the facts tell us otherwise. The good news is that the same facts also suggest that it *can* be otherwise, too.

Collective Difference and Similarity

What contribution does organic embodiment make to collective identification? In the cases of 'race' and 'disability', different patterns of individual physical differentiation – with different aetiologies and different histories – have provided bases for collective categorisations. In these cases, perniciously enduring collectivities have been conjured up from outside. In the case of 'race', the embodied differences involved have been convenient for the categorisation and abuse of entire populations. In the case of 'disability', embodied impairments are not always visible, not always disfunctional, and do not necessarily have anything in common other than their label. In each case, the end result has been an imagining of collective similarity which has channelled the distribution of resources and penalties: 'race' and 'disability' may be imagined, but in their consequences they are far from imaginary.

Men and women are more complex. In one important sense the differences aren't imagined at all: dimorphism and the physiology of reproduction are real and general throughout humanity (allowing for relatively rare physiological uncertainty). This on its own isn't enough for collective identification, however: biological sex differences characterise humanity in the abstract, but only ever individuals in the flesh. Gender differentiation, however, typified by the effective institutional and interactional dominance of men, is arguably the most ubiquitous collective classificatory principle in the human world, and enormously consequential. The detail of gender, however – unlike the detail of sexual biology – varies from group to group. Gender is thus an aspect of human collective organisation: of kinship roles, the division of labour, symbolism, and so on. In the case of differences between men and women, *individuality* can be contrasted with the *generality* of sex differences, and the *collectivity* of gender differences. Although I have argued that the biology of sex differences contributes to the ubiquity of male domination, gender, the local coding and working out of those differences, is enormously significant in the translation of biology into the observable realities of diverse hierarchical relationships between men and women.

Gender divisions are collectively defined, but they don't in themselves necessarily establish mutual recognition, obligations, or actual relationships between men or women. In any particular context they may do, but that's a matter for investigation. Unlike ethnicity or kinship, therefore, gender isn't definitively a principle of *group* formation. Unlike ethnicity or lineage, individual gender cannot be predicted from legitimate parentage. Until very recently, gender has always been a matter of individual uncertainty prior to birth, and it still depends on individual certification by others after birth. Gender is thus simultaneously individual and collective, drawing on the *general* facts of *individual* biology and the *collective* local *specifics* of gender. It's because of the interaction of these factors that, at the margins of the reproductive mainstream, sex, gender and sexuality can become so complex, varied and contested.

Gender is also massively *externally* defined. With respect to individual identification at birth, and subsequent locally appropriate practices of identification, what others think and do has an enormous impact on self-identification and how gender is experienced. Interactionally and institutionally, the gender of any individual, and its consequences, is realised through their membership of a collective category: female or male. On the other hand, however, gender − rooted as it is in the experience of being biologically female or male − is also central to self-identification, the internal point of view of embodied, individual selfhood.

Collective self-identification also depends on the imagination and assertion of a shared sense of *similarity*. Difference alone is insufficient. Although 'race' and 'disability' were, in the first instance, conjured up in the eye of the beholder, because they have become massively consequential for the people who are so categorised they may offer a basis for collective mobilisation, and political and everyday community. The embodied experience of adversity in common, and the recognition of shared interests, may gradually transform a category *in itself* into a group *for itself*.[28]

However, this process has been uneven, uncertain and fragile. In North America, for example, centuries of collective experience − African slavery, followed by systematic massive exploitation and institutionalised domination, followed by further patterns of migration from the south and across the Pacific − have created ways of life in which 'race' matters enormously and is a focus for some collective identification and expression. African-American, Asian, and Hispanic people have in common their experiences of white racism and adversity. However, this has only translated into limited collective political action.[29] On the other hand, everyday stuff such as family, language, religion and music constitutes them as different from each other within a mosaic of ethnic and 'racial' fragmentation. The bricks and mortar of their collective experiences are not the limited realities of their biological similarities and differences, and they overlap significantly with the lives and experiences of other groups, even their oppressors. 'The disabled', too, have only found a limited basis for effective collectivity in their shared categorisation:[30] impairments and embodied experiences are too diverse – deafness is utterly different from cerebral palsy, and neither has much in common with being an amputee – and there is too much else that they hold in common with the 'able-bodied'. There is, what is more, a powerful political tradition of specialised interest groups, concentrating on the amelioration of the situation of people with specific impairments, which cuts across mobilisation on more general lines.

The sharing of similar, often powerfully embodied, life-experiences also allows for the possibility that gender might be a principle of group formation or collective self-identification. The twentieth-century Women's Movement can be understood as a sustained attempt to transform individual embodied identification and categorical differentiation into collective group identification asserting similarity and shared interests. However, as the work of writers as diverse as Harriet Bradley, Beverley Skeggs and Sylvia Walby suggests,[31] the experience of being a woman, by comparison with other possibilities for group membership such as kinship, occupation, class, or ethnicity, seems to offer only a limited basis for collective identification and mobilisation.

Thus, in a manner which has some parallels with 'race' and 'disability', what women have in common with men – family, politics, language, religion, and so on – seems to count for at least as much, in the realities of significant group identification, as womanhood-in-common. The parallels are not total, however: in the case of gender, organic embodiment – and particularly the realities of fertility and reproduction – must count as *part* of an explanation if we are to understand whatever status womankind has as a real collective identification. This is so in at least two senses. First, one of the things that men and women share, which has proved an enduringly difficult issue for radical feminism in particular, is the family. It is biology – sexual enthusiasm, reproduction, the long-term dependency in body and soul of human children, and the enticing embodied otherness-to-each-other of men and women – which sets the problems to which family relationships, in all of their variability from group to group, and with all their emotional force, attempt to provide working solutions. Secondly, it can plausibly be argued that *one* of the factors on which second-wave feminism has depended for its force and success is effective contraception. The capacity of individual women, particularly under conditions of affluence, predictably to control and limit their own fertility, is as 'biological' as it is 'social' or 'cultural'. It has made an embodied difference to what it means to be in the world as a woman.

This discussion of the relationship between natural embodiment and human identification suggests several conclusions. First, individuality and collectivity may be related to each other in many different ways: there is no 'one way' here. Secondly, physiological differences and similarities, in particular, may enter into those relationships in no less various ways. Finally, the observable realities suggest that physiology offers an insecure basis for collective identification. The complex imaginings that are human symbolic universes – and intrinsic to human nature – seem to be more consequential. However, organic embodiment cannot be dismissed as irrelevant, either. Our frail and vulnerable individual bodies[32] constrain our human creativity and create the puzzles and problems to which we evolve and institutionalise collective solutions. There is more to the human world than social construction, and its limits are real.

Human Ecology

The final sense in which nature or biology matter for humans, and *vice versa*, is ecological, the relationship between humans and their natural environment. This has been an emergent theme in the discussion so far: no matter how or from which direction one approaches human nature and needs, or organically embodied difference and similarity, it's difficult to view the 'natural' and the 'social' or the 'cultural' within the kind of radical dualism that is necessary if we are confidently to defend an ontology of distinct human and natural worlds.

Even in the case of sex/gender – and I am implicitly making a case for bringing these two terms into a more intimate relationship than that in which they are usually held to be – where the biological facts of embodied organic differentiation are as general and clear as they can be, the ubiquity of male domination is not something to which these facts have *impelled* men. The realities differ from group to group. 'Male domination' is in every sociological sense an ideal type: in the real human world, real men and real women live together and apart in a variety of more or less hierarchical fashions. Most important of all, male domination is, at least in principle, capable of utter transformation, in a way that the biological facts are not (not even female fertility: this can be individually controlled, but species-wide evolutionary change would be another thing altogether). That statement may be indictable as utopian, but it isn't wrong *in fact*. As far as we know at the moment, gendered human hierarchy isn't inscribed in our genetic constitution or physiology. The capacity to make choices, and to imagine and realise alternatives, arguably is.

The wider ecology of human life points in a similar direction: can we draw a line between the human world and the natural world? The fact that, to a remarkable degree by comparison with all other animals, humans have asserted their dominion over the earth, over the bio-sphere, and over their own biologies, shouldn't be misunderstood to mean that the cut is clear between humanity and nature. The apparent triumph of world-conquering science and technology has encouraged us to treat the natural environment as something of which sociology didn't have to take account. In this context, it may be revealing that only anthropologists, studying groups with modest technological capacities and ambitions, have really taken the wider environment seriously.[33] However, now that industrialised humankind's technological achievements and attitudes to the rest of the world are coming home to roost – and our response to this has *got* to be more than just a sociology of environmental movements and risk – it's time to take our relationship with the natural world more seriously.

And the evidence that the human world is a natural world is everywhere to be found. Who of us can claim complete mastery of the range of natural responses bequeathed to each of us by our species' evolutionary history – fight or flight, blushing, sexual arousal, pain, the sheer physicality of joy and misery – and with which our bodies routinely confront us? Nor have we mastery in other senses, either: medical science notwithstanding, human bodies remain vulnerable to bacteria and viruses, to genetic mutation and damage, and to injury. Our capacity for running repairs and restoration is finite. Our bodies change naturally throughout the life course, too, letting us down as they do so. They age. At fifty, five years into reading glasses and the familial high blood pressure, my ageing is real – despite the compensatory interventions of medicine – not imagined. Finally, death waits for us all: inevitable, not the product of human construction and imagination (which isn't to deny its ever-presence in our imaginations, or the ingenuity with which we evade it). Nothing could be more natural.

Look further afield, beyond our individual bodies, and non-human nature is everywhere and even less escapable: from the surviving great cetaceans to the unimaginable mass of organisms that are invisible to the human eye, from the planetary respiration of the rain forests to the myriad plants on which we rely for sustenance. The human world, from the hidden recesses of our guts outward, is teeming with other organisms, with which we have a range of relationships – from ignorance to detailed knowledge, attempted extermination to exploitation, comfortable co-existence to domestication, avoidance to companionship – and which have considerable impact on the conditions of human life.

The weather and the seasons, too, are a perpetual backdrop to human endeavours, as is the symbiotic complexity of the planetary system on which we rely for air and water. This is, in large part, a matter of constraint and enablement, but there are senses in which human life can be said to be affected more directly. For example, some of the apparently universal human needs that I discussed earlier – shelter is an obvious example – are best understood as expressions of the interaction between human nature, our vulnerable organic embodiment and our environments. In the historical human long term, if we are properly to understand change, natural environmental patterns cannot be overlooked. Fernand Braudel, for example, in a discussion which resonates ever more loudly during a time of human-stimulated global warming, recognised climatic shifts and their relationship to population increase as a necessary part of any explanation of why capitalism took off in the early modern world.[34] In more everyday terms, much of the ingenuity that characterises the human world is a direct engagement with the environment and its hostility or constraints from an embodied human point of view. Given human nature – flexible and adaptable, exploratory, able to create artefacts, inquisitive, imaginative, highly intelligent, and capable of exercising choice – and our need for food, shelter and protection, it could not be otherwise.

Coming at this from another direction, the heavy hand of humanity lies all over the natural world. Among the most impressive human achievements – well, the biggest, anyway – are the various ways in which we have, knowingly or otherwise, modified the environment in the pursuit of our own advantage. The terraces of south-east Asian rice cultivators; the coastal salt pans of the Loire-Atlantique; the great public health civil engineering projects that transformed the experience of European city life in the nineteenth and early twentieth centuries; the vast expanse of prairie-land in North America that was produced during the course of many centuries of interaction between hunters and bison; the Panama and Suez Canals; it could be a very long list. All are human artefacts, and all provide comfortable habitats to vastly more non-humans than humans. Among the *least* impressive of human achievements, on the other hand, and perhaps the most significant environmental marks that we have yet made on the planet, are extensive terrestrial and marine pollution and climate change. The biggest human impact of all is the complex fact that there isn't a 'natural' environment anywhere on the planet today that hasn't in some respects, whether direct or indirect, been affected and transformed by human activity. There is, in fact, no separate natural world to bracket off for the purposes of sociological inquiry and analysis.

There are other reasons for being sceptical of a hard-edged distinction between the human world and the natural world that are less to do with the facts of the situation in which, as a species, we find ourselves, and more to do with the sense that we make of them. First, the notion of 'culture', which is one of the most common versions of this distinction, only really makes sense theologically, in a vision of the universe as something like a Great Chain of Being, with humanity just short of Divinity and created in His image, superior to all other living things and inert matter. Not only has this feudal image of human earthly supremacy been a precondition for environmental irresponsibility on an epic scale, but it makes no sense. Humans are not more evolved than the rest of nature.

The next reason for scepticism is that, *as a notion*, 'the natural world', somehow 'over there', is every bit a human intellectual creation.[35] In this limited sense – because whatever it is and however we think about it, the rest of the universe would continue to exist, and might even prosper, in the absence of humans – the 'natural world' is one of our own constructions. And that we *think* we have set ourselves outside nature doesn't mean that it's true: it isn't. It is proving to be a very dangerous conceit, however.[36]

Which brings me to my final argument: the anthropological realisation that there are, and have been, many human groups to whom gross distinctions between nature and humans are, or would have been, alien. Lest I be misunderstood, this is not an argument by appeal to the wisdom of the Noble Savage. It's simply an insistence that there are a multitude of human ways to understand the place of humans in the universe.[37] That which opposes nature to the human and the cultural, although it may currently be globally dominant, is only one among many. Although for centuries it has reigned supreme in the counsels of science and government in the old industrialised nations and their empires, it shouldn't be assumed that this state of affairs will continue.

Lessons for Sociology

In this chapter I've argued that the orthodox model of the place of humans in the world – on top – is ill founded, conceptually and with respect to the observable realities. I'm suggesting, instead, a model in which there *is* a human world – the world as seen, experienced and constructed by humans, individually, interactionally, and institutionally – which is also an integral part of the natural world. While this is primarily a further argument for the prosecution in the case against 'society' and 'culture', and for their supercession where possible by the model of the human world that I've been proposing throughout this book, it is also, in passing, a plea for the re-conceptualisation of the natural world.

At this point I can imagine even some of my more convinced readers asking: 'Why does this matter, *sociologically*? Can't we continue to do what we have always done, bracket off nature and biology and just get on with what sociology does best, unpacking the social construction of the human world?' It's a good question, to which the first answer is to say, yes, we *can*, and we'll still continue to do good sociology. Partial and incomplete, by my lights, but still good sociology by its own lights. Still worth doing and defending.

There are, however, good reasons why I think we *oughtn't* continue to deal with these issues by sweeping them under the carpet. There is, for example, the matter of truth. If what I have been suggesting is even partly *right*, to ignore it would be knowingly to build what we do on sand. It would leave even good sociology vulnerable to being wrong, and being seen to be wrong. It would raise questions about our ideological objectivity, and doubts about the nature of the sociological enterprise.

The arguments of this chapter should, anyway, be understood in the context of the wider arguments of the book. If there is merit in the proposal that we ought to replace the linked concepts of 'society' and 'culture' with the notion of 'the human world', then what I've suggested about the relationship between the human world and the natural world is a further argument in its favour. What's more, as I argued in Chapter Two, the analytical categories of sociological theory are utterly dependent upon our ontology of the natural world: how we analyse early-modern European accusations of witchcraft, for example, depends on whether we think it is *physically possible* for witches to fly. Our ideas about humanity and our ideas about the natural world cannot be bracketed off from each other.

Implicit in conventional sociological ontology is the radical separation between 'the socio-cultural' and 'the natural' which I am challenging. If my argument is accepted, then it's likely that sociological theory will develop in different ways than it would otherwise have done. Although it isn't my job here to predict in which ways, there are clues in the way I have discussed sex/gender, and in my argument about the human world. Other possibilities can be read in Archer's discussion of human nature, or Turner and Rojek's installation of the vulnerability of our organic embodiment at the heart of a sociological understanding of humanity.[38]

If there are to be new directions, they will emerge from debate, over time. Whatever we do, it's important to ask the right questions. Keeping 'biology'/'nature' separate from 'society'/'culture' leads us sometimes to ask the wrong questions or, even worse, to come in advance to the wrong answers. Assuming that 'disability', for example, is *only* a matter of social construction – the 'social model' argument that it is only social organisation and categorisation which translates impairment into disability, or which renders people with disabilities vulnerable – seems to me to risk not only forcing the experiences and hard-won knowledge of disabled people into the mould of our well-meant presumptions and expectations, but also to pay insufficient attention to the diversity and reality of their experiences.

Similarly, to return to relationships between men and women, without some preparedness to ask questions which invoke biology, we can either take the existing gender hierarchy for granted – as something that just *is*, like the earth beneath our feet – or we are left, in the shape of patriarchy, misogyny or sexism, with 'explanations' of male domination that, at best, require further explanations themselves. *Why* patriarchy or misogyny? Even more to the point, perhaps, if we really want to understand the differences between being in the human world as a woman or as a man – and that is something that sociologists *should* try to understand – then the day-to-day, month-to-month, year-on-year biology of fertility and sexual dimorphism is crucial (even if not determinate). In this embodied sense, men and women inhabit somewhat different, albeit hugely overlapping, human worlds.

Each of these examples suggests that social construction needs something with which to work. Those raw materials are not necessarily natural/biological – they can be utterly imagined – but they often are. And whether they are or not makes a difference. Take the trinitarian model of the human world as individual, interactional and institutional orders that I proposed in Chapter Four. Human needs, in connecting individuals who have those needs with institutions that attempt to meet those needs, offer a vivid illustration of the natural materials out of which humans construct interactively the complexity of the human world. Those materials, emerging out of the relationship between organism and environment, must be acknowledged if we are to understand better that complexity.

As a final example of asking the wrong questions, there have been, particularly with respect to ethnicity and gender, spirited debates between 'essentialists' or 'primordialists' and 'social constructionists' or 'situationalists'. To take ethnicity as an example,[39] primordialists argue that ethnic sentiments are natural, and hence an irresistible imperative which must be respected, whereas situationalists argue for the fluidity and negotiability of ethnic attachments. These are not really 'either/or' positions, however. Ethnic attachment, if it's central to earliest socialisation and subsequently reinforced, may well be a powerful individual emotional reality, difficult to see one's way out of. On the other hand, where it matters less, ethnic identification may be worn very lightly and open to change. If we accept the openness of human nature, either ethnic option lies within the 'natural' human behavioural portfolio. The theoretical framework that

I'm proposing, rather than fostering sterile debate between essentialism and social constructionism – sterile because each side knows the answer in advance – encourages a different question: given that ethnicity can be expressed and experienced with different intensities, *why* does it matter, *when* it matters? That's a matter for systematic inquiry, and an utterly sociological question.

The approach which I have begun to explore in this chapter isn't simply a matter of bolting onto generic sociology an awareness of the natural world. Just as taking feminist critique seriously in the 1970s meant more than 'adding in women', simply adding in nature won't do the trick: it'll help but it won't be enough. The mutual implication and articulation of the human and natural worlds demands a sociological rethinking of the human place in the world *and* of the natural world. Recognising that 'nature' doesn't revolve around humans – even if our sociological worldview will, necessarily, still begin with humans – means that how we see the natural world has been changed too.

The significance of this for sociological theory is potentially far-reaching. The consequences for sociological research are less easy to imagine: it's more obviously relevant to some empirical topics than others. What it shouldn't mean is that research papers or monographs will be policed to see whether the environment or human nature have received their appropriate ritual acknowledgement. More fundamentally, the foundations might be laid here for a sociology that is internally less sectarian, and externally more open to incorporating other understandings and knowledges. Since a little knowledge can be a very dangerous thing, this isn't, however, a recommendation that we should all become amateur natural scientists. Heaven forbid: we know what can happen when zoologists, for example, begin to fancy themselves as television anthropologists. More dialogue and mutual learning must be possible, however. Understanding the human world better depends on it.

One thing that isn't challenged by my proposals is the sociological commitment to a view of the human world as produced and reproduced by humans. There is no contradiction between constructionism and the attempt to understand humans as natural beings, who only do what they do in some relationship to the natural world. Quite the reverse: the capacity to construct a complex, extensive, dense and meaningful world – a human world – is integral to human nature. However, without an appreciation of the natural constraints within which that work proceeds, and of the full range of natural materials on which it draws and which it uses, social constructionism is impoverished and introverted. This isn't just a matter of sociological importance, either: in the face of the pervasive biological determinism of common sense and science, a tough-minded, defensible constructionist perspective remains as necessary as ever.

Seven
Why Sociology Matters

There would have been no point in writing this book if I didn't believe that sociology matters. If for no other reason, sociology matters to me because it is definitively a critical activity. In the words of Tom Burns, during his inaugural lecture at the University of Edinburgh: 'The practice of sociology is criticism. It exists to criticise claims about the values of achievement and to question assumptions about the meaning of conduct. It is the business of sociologists to conduct a critical debate with the public about its equipment of social institutions.'[1] These words remain as true today as when they were first uttered in the middle of the 1960s. The critical attitude which I think Burns had in mind, and in the spirit of which this book is written, isn't necessarily in the service of any specific desired future, nor is it criticism for its own sake. It is potentially more subversive than either: criticism which simply cannot help itself by virtue of its alternative understandings of the world of humans.

What Matters...

Among the alternatives which I have explored in this book is a heterodox view of the discipline of sociology. Where in our present systems of higher education we typically have separate disciplinary departments – usually in separate buildings, sometimes even in separate faculties – I see nothing but a unified intellectual field, albeit fractured by institutional histories and the necessity of specialisation. This *generic sociology* has at its core the intellectual activities and concerns of social and cultural anthropology, social history, social psychology, and sociology, and also includes a good deal of what goes on within social and public policy, cultural studies, human geography, women's studies, and so on. Comfortable among neither the sciences nor the humanities – too imprecise for one lot, too empirically systematic for the others – its core business of understanding pattern in human behaviour is organised around the linked themes of change and the relationship between individuals and collectivities. In continuing to pursue these questions, sociology remains true to its origins in the great upheavals of the nineteenth century.

Anybody who claims to understand, or even to be *trying* to understand, humans and what they do is immediately faced with competitive expert opinion in the shape of everyday common sense. The world isn't full of 'lay sociologists' – that idea has always been a somewhat self-centred sociological smugness – but it is full of people with at least a plausible claim to know better than we do: because it's them we're talking about, because they were there, because they know something we don't know, or because, well, who do *we* think we are, telling them what *their* lives mean? One of the most urgent tasks for sociologists, in terms both of how they see themselves and of how others see them, has always been to establish a legitimate, defensible claim to know better than common sense.

For the sociology that I am advocating, unwilling to assume a privileged epistemological status, unable to presume to the dubious authority of science, and keen to communicate in as clear and accessible a fashion as possible, this task is even more urgent. There are three arguments which justify sociology's claim to understand the human world better than the various versions of common sense:

- *systematic inquiry* allows sociology to draw on a wider and more detailed array of facts than common sense;
- relative *objectivity* should permit sociology to come to a view of any situation which is independent of the goals and demands of protagonists; and
- sociological *theory* encourages the particular and the general to be seen in the context of each other.

Although sociological sense differs from common sense in these respects, the two are in some respects closer than might be expected. For instance, the ways by which sociologists find out about the human world are not so strikingly different from the ways everyone else does, when shopping, or catching a bus, on holiday, or whatever. Because sociology is, or ought to be, 'empirically responsible',[2] doing sociological research means gathering information *more systematically* than we can afford or usually need to in everyday life. However, the epistemological assumptions on the basis of which we operate are very similar in either case. We couldn't get on with everyday living or collecting research data without assuming the existence of observable realities, about which it is possible to know, and about which it is possible to make plausible, defensible generalisations. This is *everyday realism*.

Given this stance, what matters is how we defend the plausibility of our claims to knowledge. There are two aspects to this, the first of which deals with the observable realities. In Chapter Five I suggested that for sociologists there are six kinds of primary data: basic numbers, what people say, everything else that people do, intentionally communicative artefacts, other artefacts, and the human shaping and organisation of the physical environment. All of these can, in principle, be known, and all are sociologically significant, the more so when they are brought together. The second dimension of the sociological claim to be able to know – and to know *better* – depends upon the systematicity of sociological inquiry. This demands that our research activities should be sensible, comprehensive, transparent and sceptical. Arguably these criteria apply to all kinds of research, and they allow us to make a plausible claim to knowledge of the facts.

Sociological research involves documenting those facts and the common sense or senses that they make in situational context, and subsequently making sociological sense of the data within theoretical, explanatory models which permit generalisation and comparison. One of the most unambiguous aspects of my vision of generic sociology is that it neither encourages 'pure' theory, undisciplined by the evidence provided by systematic inquiry, nor accepts that research can be done in the absence of theory. If we are to have a viable sociology, properly engaged with the realities of which it claims knowledge, theory and research are not separable activities. While it is a commonplace of sociological conventional wisdom that research without theory is impossible, at best – and regrettably – the reverse stricture seems to apply only weakly to much theorising.

Given the centrality to sociology of systematic inquiry, and the nature of its primary data, what is the bigger picture into which they have to be fitted, and toward which they contribute? This is the question of sociology's basic subject matter, what it's *about*. I have suggested that the concepts of 'society' and 'culture', on which sociology seems to depends for a sense of this bedrock, are no more than different ways of talking about the same things:

- the more-than-the-sum-of-the-parts that is such a powerful, albeit somewhat elusive, human reality;
- the reality of more-or-less bounded human groups; and
- established and organised human interaction and ways of doing things.

If my argument in this respect is accepted, the conceptual distinction between 'society' and 'culture' is redundant. More than that, however, these concepts are fundamentally misleading. First, the distinction between them does unnecessary violence to the messy integrity of human experience and collective organisation. The observable reality is simply that there is no such ontological distinction: the 'social' and the 'cultural', and the differences between them, are neither obvious in the real world nor even conceptually easy to tease apart. Secondly, 'society' and 'culture' are typically conceptualised as collective dimensions of human life, in opposition to individuals and individuality. This reifies both individuality *and* collectivity, passing over or ignoring the necessary implication of each in the other and distorting the nature of human life and experience in the process. On the one hand, individuality is over-emphasised at the expense of the collective, intersubjective formation and functioning of embodied individuals. On the other, the routinely imprecise, permeable, shifting and flexible character of collective boundaries isn't recognised. It is the worst of both possible worlds. Finally, these notions are historically specific (grounded in the political and intellectual projects of eighteenth- and nineteenth-century Europe and North America) rather than generally applicable.

For these reasons, I am proposing that sociology should wherever possible stop talking about 'society' and 'culture'. While this may not always be possible, there are good substitutes available in 'the collective', 'collectivity' and 'collectivities', and in the notion of the 'human world' – or 'the world of humans' – that I'm proposing as sociology's fundamental subject matter. This is the world with humans in it, produced and reproduced by humans, and seen from a human standpoint. It's a world inhabited by embodied individuals, who act with others or in orientation towards others, and who are identified, at least in part, by their membership, with other humans, of collectivities of various sorts. In this understanding of human experience and organisation, the individual and the collective necessarily co-exist and are not opposed to each other. Human individuals and collectivities cannot be human without each other.

The expression, 'the human world' may not be particularly elegant – although I hope that the previous chapters have shown that it isn't horribly problematic, either – but it doesn't buy into the problematic distinction between the social and the cultural. It places embodied human beings unmistakably at the heart of sociology. In this I hope that it avoids the trap, into which we can fall simply through our use of language, of reifying the more-than-the-sum-of-the-parts as something above individuals and against them, acting on them, somehow existing 'over their heads' or 'behind their backs'. Whereas society and culture are collective and somewhat abstract notions, 'the human world' only invokes collectivity at the same time as it acknowledges actual, existing individuals. It is a real world: full of real people, of the collective co-presence of active humans, dealing with each other and producing and reproducing their world, whether they intend to or not. To talk about the human world is therefore to reject static models of structure and system, and to embrace the routine flexibility and movement of human life. Although the human world is not in any sense *reducible* to embodied individuals – it is, after all, an attempt to think about the more-than-sum-of-the-parts of human life – it is *constituted* of, in, and by them.

If this was all there was to it the idea of the human world would – at best – be of interest only to the 'decorative'[3] general theorists of whom I have been so critical. However, as a way of thinking about the *real* world, it's also intended to be relevant to the business of doing empirical research. Intrinsic to its formulation is the proposal that the observable realities of the human world can be thought about in three different ways:

- as an *individual order* of embodied individuals and what-goes-on-in-their-heads;
- as an *interaction order* of relationships between individuals, what-goes-on-between-people; and
- as an *institutional order* of pattern and organisation, established-ways-of-doing-things.

The terminology here is partly chosen as a reminder that the human world is ordered, even if it isn't always orderly. Empirically, each of these 'orders' can be 'found' in, and can shed light on, any of the six kinds of primary data referred to above. Nor are the observable realities involved mysterious: embodied individuals exist, we can participate in and observe interaction, and institutionalised ways of doing things survive over time and have substance in human knowledge, assemblies, artefacts, and patterns of behaviour.

Primary data notwithstanding, however, these are *classificatory* orders. They should not be confused with the real places, people and things of the human world. The individual, interactional and institutional orders – unlike individuals, interaction and institutions – are not observable realities. They are ideal-typical models, which help us conceptualise the human world and its complexity. They can facilitate the organisation and interpretation of our data, and allow for concrete thinking about the elusive more-than-the-sum-of-the-parts.

While the individual, interactional and institutional orders can be thought of separately, the real individuals, interaction, and institutions that they help us to think about are the indissoluble trinity which constitutes the more-than-the-sum-of-the-parts of the human world. Conceptually, they occupy the same space (the human world) and are at the same time distinct (in the individual, interactional and institutional orders). Since, as observable realities, individuals, interaction and institutions are only based on and constituted in real embodied humans, they also overlap in everyday physical space. Individuals, interaction, and institutions necessarily co-exist: we need each of them to make sense of the others.

Finally, to revisit the argument of the previous chapter, not only does the human world encompass the accumulated materiality of human technology and artefacts, but it can also be understood as part of the 'natural world'. While 'the natural world' and 'the human world' are not the same, they are arguably different perspectives on the world in which humans find themselves, and of which they are a part. Humans are 'natural' organisms, with a nature and needs, enabled and constrained by their bodies, in necessary ecological relationships with a wider non-human environment over which they have only limited control. Organic human-ness is significant if we are to understand what humans do and the human world. Sociology has been too long in denial about this.

Although humans have relentlessly attempted to master their physical environment, that environment reacts back upon the human world – there is no insulation between the two – with individual, interactional and institutional consequences for humans. The natural world is the framework of possibilities and impossibilities within which the human world exists. If this is true, sociology cannot claim to understand the human world without at least acknowledging the relevance of the natural world. In this respect, a further argument for the approach that

I'm proposing – which, by virtue of its rejection of the usefulness of the notion of 'culture', doesn't espouse a culture–nature dualism – is that it might encourage sociology to adopt a genuinely ecological perspective on the relationship between humans and their wider environment.

Why it Matters...

Whether my rethinking of the sociological foundations matters depends in part on what sociology's future might be. One useful constraint on any attempt to think about the future is the uncomfortable truth that our present situation is really only as durable as it eventually turns out to be, which can only be known with benefit of hindsight. Who in the year 1900, for example, would have imagined that one hundred years later nearly every large British city would have at least two universities, or that something called 'sociology' would be a substantial activity in most of them? Or that the natural sciences should have become endangered activities in terms of undergraduate teaching? Hubris and complacency are ever-present temptations, which only an effort to imagine a range of optimistic *and* pessimistic futures can defend against.

The arguments for a genuinely generic sociology appear stronger and more pressing in this context. The more flexibility and room for manoeuvre we allow ourselves, the better we can respond to changing circumstances. The more broadly we define our discipline, the more likely we are to be able to defend it, and the less likely we are to dissolve slowly into cultural studies, women's studies, ethnic studies, and so on. A broadly-based, open-bordered approach such as the one that I'm proposing seems to be the most likely guarantor of our intellectual future.

In terms of *realpolitik*, however, I recognise that generic sociology is an unlikely, even utopian, institutional prospect in the short term. I have too much respect for the solidity of established departmental boundaries, the ferocity of vested and competitive interests, and the drag of organisational and individual inertia, to be too carried away by my own optimistic vision. Within these constraints, however, those of us who wish to can work to establish working intellectual agreements about what we have in common and build co-operative relationships on the back of them. The elementary model of the human world that I have put forward here offers the common ground, and the basic foundations, on which to do that building. My own experience of having one foot in sociology and the other in social anthropology doesn't lead me to believe that this will be easy, but it is nevertheless *possible*. Certainly an intellectually open and permissive basic model of the human world, and how we are to understand it, should be a help rather than a hindrance.

Turning to my arguments for the model of the human world that I am proposing, these don't, however – and thank goodness – derive from academic or institutional priorities. The world is changing, as ever, and we need to change with it. Take, for example, John Urry's prognosis of the increasing flexibility and declining significance of the boundaries of nation-state 'societies'.[4] If he turns out to be even partly correct, it can only be another argument for adopting a model of sociology's fundamental subject matter which is built on a minimum of preconceptions.

The model of the human world that I have presented in this book, presuming only the existence of individuals, interaction and institutions, fits the bill in this respect: it works satisfactorily on the basis of very few constituent conceptual parts. It's also likely to be a good deal less ethnocentric than the modernist sociology that Urry is criticising. If we are to attempt to understand the diversity of human worlds, whether in the past, the present or the future, and to recognise the similarities as well as the differences between human collectivities and individuals, we require a robust, general-purpose ontology of the human world such as the one that I am proposing.

The globalisation of human collectivities isn't the only significant change on the horizon. Environmental change isn't even on the horizon: in our everyday experience of the weather it's overhead, right now. Whether one prefers the better or worse case scenarios, all of our likely futures suggest that we will no longer be able to persist in the comfortable misconceptualisation of the human world as insulated from, and dominating, the physical environment. This illusion has probably only ever been sustainable from the point of view of the prosperous industrial nations – the same nations that can afford well-founded sociology departments – so ethnocentricity is an issue here too. The confidence that humanity had successfully declared its independence of the natural global system is one of the many conceits of modernism. We need to reinsert the human world into nature if we are to continue to claim any significance for what we do. In the process we may also, in a small way, contribute to the development of whatever new take on the world – human and natural – will allow humanity to build on and move beyond modernity. Any offers for a *genuine* postmodernity?

Nor is 'the environment' all there is to nature. Humans are organisms with an embodied human nature, albeit plastic and permissive, with needs, and with some enormously consequential *real* differences between us that are neither imagined nor constructed. If we are successfully to resist the excesses of biological determinism and assert the virtues of a constructionist approach, burying our heads in the sand about our own biology doesn't seem likely to be a particularly effective strategy. It hasn't helped sociology to be taken seriously in these debates so far. For humans as organisms, change is afoot across a range of fronts, all of which offer challenges, and to all of which sociology ought to attend. Whether the viruses and bacteria of the world continue to bite back at the human hand that once thought it had them contained, if not on the run, or we step into the brave new world promised by advances in genetics, we will no longer be able to quarantine the biology of human being and embodiment within brackets, not if we wish to cling to any relevance at all.

To fold this discussion back into the everyday human world before moving on, there is one last reason – perhaps the most important – why sociology matters. My account of sociology and its possibilities is grounded in an appreciation of the collective dimensions of the human world. It's the more-than-the-sum-of-the-parts of the human world which gives sociology its distinctive intellectual mission and makes the sociological game worth playing. This is more than an intellectual matter, however. It is vital that we understand and affirm the collective realities of human existence if we are to defend our humanity in the face of the materialist individualism which is increasingly the dominant value framework of global capitalism.

At the risk of shoehorning the arguments and positions of others into my own, and distorting or trivialising what they have to say in the process, what I call materialist individualism bears more than a passing resemblance to what Jules Henry described as 'pecuniary logic'.[5] It resembles closely the enemy which Alasdair MacIntyre has in his sights in his defence of virtue and values against the hegemony of reason.[6] This also makes it the opposite of the solidarity and belonging which Bryan Turner and Chris Rojek propose as the proper theme of sociology.[7] When George Ritzer, for example, talks about the need to re-enchant the modern world,[8] he isn't a million miles from where I am standing, and nor is Zygmunt Bauman's recent cautious rediscovery of the virtues of community, or his proposal to 'recall universalism from exile'.[9] Finally, the particular version of common sense which Ralph Fevre blames for the 'demoralization of western culture' – by which he means an attitude towards others founded on reason and immediate knowledge rather than the possibility of trust or faith in either them or one's own judgement[10] – is at least a close cousin of my materialist individualism.

I don't cite these authors here to endorse them all. I am arguing for an empirically responsible and firmly rationalist sociology, so I can imagine grounds for disagreement with some of them. The job description of sociology has always, historically, included the disenchantment of the human world as one of its central functions. That's still the case and I don't think it can or should be otherwise. Insisting that 'there is such a thing as society' is all very well: it is the particular responsibility of sociology to *show* what the more-than-the-sum-of-the-parts of the human world is, and to *demonstrate* that as human beings we simply cannot do without it. Faith and trust are no more sufficient in this respect than reason and the evidence of our senses. However, at the very least this literature suggests that my general argument may increasingly be flowing with, rather than standing against, a gathering tide.

Making it Matter ...

None of the above will be to much effect if we don't do something about our relationship with the fee-paying public. There is very little written by sociologists to vie with the kind of genuine and praiseworthy popularisation – wide appeal without dumbing down – that natural scientists, psychologists and historians manage on occasions to achieve. Despite the nature of our subject matter, which one might think should guarantee us a modicum of popular attention, we talk to each other a great deal more than we engage in the critical debate with the public demanded by Tom Burns. Since sociology, whether it be teaching or research, is almost totally reliant on public or charitable funding, this is no small matter.

What is the problem here? First of all, do we really *know* stuff, about which we can tell the world with confidence? My argument in Chapter Five suggests that we are in a position to insist that we *do* know something, quite a lot in fact, about the human world. This is not just a matter of being able to parade a sequence of competitive accounts or representations of that world. There is a body of sociological *knowledge* to which we can lay claim with some confidence. After a century or more of generic sociology, this is substantial. Even if no-one else does, historians of the future will have considerable reason to thank us for our labours.

Next, there may be some doubt about whether what we know would be interesting to a broad public. While this criterion can't, of course, be held up as the only yardstick of value, it isn't irrelevant, either. We may not be in the business of making headline-grabbing discoveries, but the good news is that much of what we do is intrinsically – not narrowly sociologically –

interesting. It's about health and illness, about religion, about globalisation, about generational changes and experiences, about changing gender roles, about tourism, about the people and places that most tourism glosses over, about identity, about the changing ways in which we make our livings, about sexuality, and about many other things beside. If we ever become serious about incorporating into sociology a thoroughgoing ecological perspective on the human–natural world, that list can only get longer.

There are, however, a number of reasons why we sociologists are not realising our potential in this market. Perhaps the most obvious is our use of language. This has been discussed so often that little will be served by going over that ground here. Nor do I intend to seize on some spectacularly incomprehensible quotations, carefully selected from high-visibility miscreants, to grill over the coals of my superiority and wit. If there are readers who don't already accept that a great deal of sociological writing is unclear, long-winded, pretentious, ponderous, over-burdened with jargon, and no pleasure to read, then my trans-lating a few titbits into clear English won't change their minds. Referring them to C. Wright Mills, Stanislav Andreski or Howard Becker probably wouldn't work either.[11] The best that I can do is to write clearly and show that we don't have to abandon words like 'epistemology' or deny ourselves theory in order to communicate accessibly. If that were true, there would be no point.

This problem has several roots. First, we are too accustomed to talking to each other. Not only can we get away with our own groupspeak, but, since so many of us are in the same boat, we are insufficiently critical of each other in this respect (if no other). The result is a vicious circle of mutual obscurantism. Secondly, too much of what's published as sociology is the muddled thinking of a theoretical discourse that isn't subject to the discipline which derives from systematic inquiry and attention to the details of observable reality. This can't possibly encourage clarity of thinking or expression. Thirdly, there is the seduc-tive allure of profundity and Cultural gravitas. Big words, big sentences and big paragraphs are often mistaken for big thinking, and complicated clause structure for complicated ideas. In fact there's probably an inverse relationship between these things. Finally, the classic *ex cathedra* style of academic detachment – no first person, extensive use of the passive tense, and so on – is still encouraged throughout secondary and higher education. It isn't necessary, and it's no substitute for the authority which derives from actually knowing what we're talking about.

The clarity with which we communicate is an ethical issue as much as anything else. It's about how we discharge the responsibilities that we have to the other inhabitants of the human world, who, in every sense, provide us with our livings. Too much sociological writing is an intimidatory and inexcusable affront to those responsibilities. If no-one else, our students – who are, after all, our best and most immediate audience – are owed better than we give them in this respect.

The perceived lack of objectivity of much of what we say may be another handicap in the eyes of a wider readership. The uncomfortable reality is that, particularly in terms of research, it's not always possible to remain objective: pressures against objectivity come from the demands and needs of the agency that is directly funding the research, of whoever the research is about, and, not least, of the researcher. All of these demands and needs are in their own way legitimate to a point. Objectivity is, therefore, a permanent aspiration, rather than a state of grace that we can definitely attain.

Recognising the force of these pressures, however, I am unconvinced that we've done the best possible job to defend the limited and precious objectivity that we can claim. For example, too often we have succumbed to the argument that objectivity is a misleading myth – not only impossible, but a dangerous notion – and chosen righteousness, or straightforward sectional politics, rather than an open-minded and difficult engagement with the observable realities. If for no other reason, this matters because it is a matter of the facts, of *truth*. This doesn't have to involve something as dramatic as the outright suppression or fabrication of evidence, either (although the examples of Freud and Burt should never be far from our minds[12]). As in recent controversies about the reality and prevalence of satanic abuse,[13] the most serious problem may be self-referential frameworks of ideas and politics which are in the business of confirming rather than testing their worldviews, and which decide *a priori* what counts as admissible evidence and explanation.

As I argued in Chapter One, objectivity is at its most important if we do espouse politics and values which inform our choice of research topics and interests. Doing the best possible job to establish the truth – as close as we can get to it – no matter how inconvenient, is surely the only basis for answering the question, still as urgent as when Lenin posed it, 'What is to be done?' If we want our work to be trusted outside the narrow circuits of the discipline, as something other than ideology, vested interest or common sense in disguise, it's absolutely vital. If my diagnosis is right, this will, I realise, be difficult to deal with: it's much easier to look the other way.

Finally, the perceived tone and tenor of sociology probably doesn't do the discipline many favours either. What I'm about to say doesn't apply to everything that might be counted as generic sociology – anthropology, for example, has for long periods suffered from the opposite malaise – but it does have some general applicability. This point harks back to C. Wright Mills and his notion of 'public issues and private problems'. Not only has sociology long been problem- and issue-oriented, but as one of the definitive voices of disenchanting and disenchanted modernist rationalism – which, to repeat myself, is as it should be – it often appears somewhat gloomy, if not downright miserable. Seen from the outside, it's often all disadvantage, deviance and human misery, and with all the illusions apparently stripped away. These matters are, of course, important, but they are not the sum total of human existence. And, thank goodness, sociology has changed a good deal in recent decades. Many sociologists today adopt a different style – fortunately not always under the sign of postmodernism – and our research portfolio has broadened considerably.[14] There may, however, be a lag in public perceptions, which it is up to sociologists to address.

This brings the wheel full circle, to how we should address the public, and to the role of sociology in encouraging intellectual democracy. I want to close by agreeing with Dorothy Smith, that if we are to have a sociology for the twenty-first century it should be 'a sociology for people', a sociology which has its starting point in the realities of life for real people, actual individuals.[15] In a world that is complex and getting more so, and taking into account the limitations of common sense as a means of grasping and understanding that complexity, a sociology that is genuinely *in* and *of* the human world has much to offer.

This suggests that the real – certainly the biggest – job for sociology is education for active citizenship. If you prefer, this could also be described as education for positive and constructive resistance to the control which is inherent in citizenship. *Seeing* that control is the first and perhaps most important point. As well as better empirical knowledge of the human world and how it works, this might include:

- the skills of systematic inquiry, to help people find things out for themselves;
- the analytical skills to help them work things out for themselves;
- the critical vigilance to encourage them to do both; and
- the openness to encourage them to attempt to understand the new and the different.

In other words, the sociological point is not, in the first instance, to change the world, but rather to understand it. Change *may* be a likely outcome, but that's a different matter. To put this in another way, perhaps Marx never understood that since it's organically embodied, active humans who do the understanding – not free-floating intellects – understanding the human world necessarily implies at least the prospect of changing it. This is why teaching is still sociology's most important and most defensible activity.

Active citizenship can also be understood in terms of individual reflexivity. While sociology's contribution to reflexive personal development is more difficult to pin down than its role in fostering citizenship, it is, however, at least as important. It's a matter of seeing things in a different way, of 'thinking sociologically' in Bauman's sense, of developing an individual sociological imagination. It's a matter of acquiring a sociological point of view on the human world. This isn't a dramatic conversion experience – a sociological road to Damascus – but a gradual process of supplementing what is already known and understood with complementary sociological sense. A process of coming to see the relationship between the individual and the collective, and the reciprocal implication of each in the unfolding and working out of change.

That doesn't *have* to happen, of course. It certainly doesn't happen to everyone who studies sociology. For the many students who approach sociology in a more or less instrumental fashion it's probably the last thing that they want, and that's fine. But for many other students, studying sociology marks a change in their point of view on the human world, a small process of transformation in their lives.

What is that changed point of view? First of all it involves *seeing* 'the human world' for yourself. It's an approach to explaining the human world not just in terms of the behaviour and characteristics of individuals but also in terms of wider social situations and general themes or principles. It is, whenever possible, comparative across different contexts and situations. It doesn't accept things at face value. Its interpretations are offered on the basis of a sceptical and systematic appraisal of the available evidence about the observable realities. It is definitely in the business of making connections between things, and trying to understand what those connections mean. And, last but not least, it attempts to be detached or objective.

This, it seems to me, is the true value of what sociology has to offer, and you don't have to be a working sociologist to buy into it. Not everyone will find it useful, of course, particularly in that it has the potential to undermine ideology's blurring of the *is* and the *ought*. The critical eye of sociology may make life awkward and uncomfortable. Indeed, it absolutely *should*. However, in that occasional awkwardness and discomfort lies the potential to enrich how we see the world and perhaps to make it easier rather than more difficult to live with its complexities.

Finally, to come back to citizenship, the sociological point of view can also make a general contribution to the character of the human world and the experience of living in it. Sociology originally developed because people in the nineteenth century wanted to understand better the rapid changes that were taking place in the human world. That world is still changing, and we still need to understand better what's going on. As Giddens among others has pointed out,[16] as an integral part of modern humanity's attempt to understand itself, sociology necessarily feeds back into the human world. Viewed in this way, sociology is something we can't live without. It's in the background and in the foreground of the modern world. If we are to remain committed to ideals such as democracy and active citizenship – no matter how tarnished they may appear in the mouths of many of their loudest advocates – then we *really* can't live without it.

Notes

Notes to Chapter One: Foundations of Sociology

1. C. Wright Mills, *The Sociological Imagination* (New York: Oxford University Press, 1959).

2. A. W. Gouldner, *The Coming Crisis of Western Sociology* (London: Heinemann, 1971) p. 7. See also A. W. Gouldner, *For Sociology: Renewal and Critique in Sociology Today* (London: Allen Lane, 1973).

3. S. Andreski, *Social Sciences as Sorcery* (London: André Deutsch, 1972).

4. There are very many examples I could cite here. I will stick to three: J. Mitchell and A. Oakley (eds), *The Rights and Wrongs of Women* (Harmondsworth: Penguin, 1976); D. E. Smith, *The Everyday World as Problematic: A Feminist Sociology* (Milton Keynes: Open University Press, 1988); and L. Stanley and S. Wise, *Breaking Out: Feminist Consciousness and Feminist Research* (London: Routledge and Kegan Paul, 1983).

5. J. H. Goldthorpe, *On Sociology: Numbers, Narratives and the Integration of Research and Theory* (Oxford: Oxford University Press, 2000) p. 1.

6. For an overview of some of these critiques, see S. R. Quah and A. Sales, 'Of Consensus, Tension and Sociology at the Dawn of the 21st Century', in S. R. Quah and A. Sales (eds), *The International Handbook of Sociology* (London: Sage, 2000).

7. Other comments on the disconnection between general theory and empirical research include P. Bourdieu and L. J. D. Wacquant, *An Invitation to Reflexive Sociology* (Cambridge: Polity Press, 1992) pp. 174–6, 218–24; B. S. Turner, 'Preface' to B. S. Turner (ed.), *The Blackwell Companion to Social Theory*, 2nd edn (Oxford: Blackwell, 2000).

8. On what Peter Berger, in *Invitation to Sociology: A Humanistic Introduction* (Harmondsworth: Pelican, 1966) p. 25, called sociology's 'barbaric dialect', see S. Andreski, *Social Sciences as Sorcery*, pp. 59–88; H. S. Becker, *Writing for Social Scientists* (Chicago: University of Chicago Press, 1986); R. Jenkins, *Pierre Bourdieu* (London: Routledge, 1992) pp. 9–10, 162–72; C. Wright Mills, *The Sociological Imagination*, pp. 25–35, 217–22.

9. It isn't only hard-nosed quantitative sociologists who recognise the need to strive for epistemological objectivity: Z. Bauman, *Thinking Sociologically* (Oxford: Blackwell, 1990), pp. 5–6; P. L. Berger, *Invitation to Sociology*, pp. 27–9; S. Bruce, *Sociology: A Very Short Introduction* (Oxford: Oxford University Press, 1999) pp. 94–112.

10. Z. Bauman, *Thinking Sociologically*, p. 3.

11. B. S. Turner, 'Preface' to B. S. Turner (ed.), *The Blackwell Companion to Social Theory*, p. xiv. For a wider critique of 'decorative sociology', see B. S. Turner and C. Rojek, *Society and Culture: Principles of Scarcity and Solidarity* (London: Sage, 2001).

12. In much sociological writing, 'methodology' refers to data-gathering procedures. This is wrong: these are research *methods*. This is a good example of the sociological abuse of language, perhaps in an attempt to invoke the mantle of maximum (scientific) authority.

13. Here is an example of how difficult it is to divorce methodology and ontology: 'I seek to avoid any such difficulty by starting from an acceptance of methodological – though not ontological – individualism: that is, from the position that all social phenomena can and should *be explained as* resulting from the action and interaction of individuals. Thus, the theory that I shall try to develop will be one that aims to show how ... macrosocial regularities ... *are the outcome* of such action and interaction. ... I shall indeed make reference ... to institutions or other social structural features. ... None the less, the assumption remains that these features too are no more than *the product* of past action and its consequences' (J. H. Goldthorpe, *On Sociology*, pp. 164–5; my italics). How quickly a mode of *explanation* becomes a statement about the *nature* of the phenomena being explained, and methodology becomes ontology.

14. G. McLennan, 'The New Positivity', in J. Eldredge *et al.* (eds), *For Sociology: Legacies and Prospects* (Durham: Sociology Press, 2000); D. Silverman, 'Telling Convincing Stories: A Plea for Cautious Positivism in Case-Studies', in B. Glassner and J. D. Moreno (eds), *The Quantitative – Qualitative Distinction in the Social Sciences* (The Hague: Kluwer, 1989).

15. For an introduction to debates about objectivity, see W. Outhwaite, 'The Philosophy of Social Science', in B. S. Turner (ed.), *The Blackwell Companion to Social Theory*, especially pp. 60–3.

16. M. Weber, *The Methodology of the Social Sciences*, ed. E. A. Shils and H. A. Finch (New York: Free Press, 1949); and 'Science as a Vocation', in H. H. Gerth and C. Wright Mills (eds), *From Max Weber: Essays in Sociology* (London: Routledge and Kegan Paul, 1948).

17. For example: S. Harding (ed.), *Feminism and Methodology: Social Science Issues* (Bloomington: Indiana University Press, 1987), especially the chapters by Smith, Hartmann, MacKinnon and Hartsock. On 'emancipatory research' see the special issue of *Disability, Handicap and Society*, vol. 7 (1992) no. 4.

18. M. Weber, *The Protestant Ethic and the Spirit of Capitalism*, 2nd edn (London: George Allen and Unwin, 1976) p. 182.

19. See the arguments of Bauman and Berger cited in note 9, above.

20. This famous remark is from the *Theses on Feuerbach* (1845), which are widely available in anthologies of Marx's writings.

21. For an example of the tortuous paths down which materialist determinism led, and the degree to which the real world had to be renounced, see L. Althusser, *Lenin and Philosophy, and Other Essays* (London: Verso, 1971) especially pp. 127–86.

22. On our reluctance to acknowledge biology in discussing relationships between men and women, see T. Lovell, 'Feminisms of the Second Wave' and 'Feminism Transformed?', in B. S. Turner (ed.), *The Blackwell Companion to Social Theory*.

23. *Pro* rational action theory, see J. H. Goldthorpe, *On Sociology*, pp. 94–136. *Contra*, see P. Bourdieu, *The Logic of Practice* (Cambridge: Polity Press, 1990) pp. 46–51; and P. Bourdieu and L. J. D. Wacquant, *An Invitation to Reflexive Sociology*, pp. 123–6.

24. A. Giddens, *In Defence of Sociology: Essays, Interpretations and Rejoinders* (Cambridge: Polity, 1996).

25. See note 8 to this chapter, above.

26. For example: G. Ritzer, *The McDonaldization of Society: An Investigation into the Changing Character of Contemporary Social Life* (Thousand Oaks: Pine Forge Press, 1993); R. Sennett, *The Corrosion of Character: The Personal Consequences of Work in the New Capitalism* (New York: W. W. Norton, 1998).

27. On sociology as a worldview, see S. Restivo, *The Sociological Worldview* (Cambridge, Mass.: Blackwell, 1991).

28. A notion of 'generic sociology' has also been used and promoted by Gregor McLennan, in 'The New Positivity', cited above.

Notes to Chapter Two: What is Sociology?

1. F. Tönnies, *Community and Association* (London: Routledge and Kegan Paul, 1955 [1887]); E. Durkheim, *The Division of Labour in Society* (London: Macmillan, 1984 [1893]); G. Simmel, 'The Metropolis and Mental Life', in K. H. Wolff (ed.), *The Sociology of Georg Simmel* (New York: Free Press, 1950).

2. E. Durkheim, *The Division of Labour in Society*; and *Suicide: A Study in Sociology* (London: Routledge and Kegan Paul, 1952 [1897]); M. Weber, 'Science as a Vocation', 'The Social Psychology of the World Religions' and 'The Protestant Sects and the Spirit of Capitalism', in H. H. Gerth and C. Wright Mills (eds), *From Max Weber: Essays in Sociology* (London: Routledge and Kegan Paul, 1948).

3. A. Giddens (ed.), *Emile Durkheim: Selected Writings* (Cambridge: Cambridge University Press, 1972) pp. 203–18.

4. B. Ballis Lal, 'The "Chicago School" of American Sociology, Symbolic Interactionism, and Race Relations Theory', in J. Rex and D. Mason (eds), *Theories of Race and Ethnic Relations* (Cambridge: Cambridge University Press, 1986); and *The Romance of Culture in an Urban Civilization: Robert E. Park on Race and Ethnic Relations in Cities* (London: Routledge, 1990).

5. See the works of G. W. Stocking: *Race, Culture and Evolution* (New York: Free Press, 1968); *Victorian Anthropology* (New York: Free Press, 1987); and his recent edited collection, *Colonial Situations* (Madison: University of Wisconsin Press, 1991).

6. J. H. Goldthorpe, *On Sociology: Numbers, Narratives and the Integration of Research and Theory* (Oxford: Oxford University Press, 2000) pp. 4–6, 259–60. For an account of the relationship between sociology and science which differs from the one I offer, see M. Williams, *Science and Social Science: An Introduction* (London: Routledge, 2000).

7. See M. Weber, *The Protestant Ethic and the Spirit of Capitalism*, 2nd edn (London: George Allen & Unwin, 1976) p. 182.

8. I. A. Richter (ed.), *The Notebooks of Leonardo da Vinci* (Oxford: Oxford University Press, 1952) p. 9.

9. M. S. Archer, 'The Dubious Guarantees of Social Science: a Reply to Wallerstein', *International Sociology*, vol. 13 (1998) pp. 5–17.

10. A. Giddens, *Runaway World: How Globalisation is Reshaping Our Lives* (Cambridge: Polity Press, 1999).

11. C. Wright Mills, *The Sociological Imagination* (New York: Oxford University Press, 1959) p. 77.

12. A. Schutz, *The Phenomenology of the Social World* (Evanston: Northwestern University Press, 1972) pp. 215–50; and A. Schutz and T. Luckmann, *The Structures of the Life-World* (Evanston: Northwestern University Press, 1973) pp. 3–20. Apropos Bourdieu, see R. Jenkins, *Pierre Bourdieu* (London: Routledge, 1992) pp. 45–65.

13. C. Wright Mills, *The Sociological Imagination*, pp. 8–11.

14. Ibid., pp. 76–99, 195–226.

15. Z. Bauman, *Thinking Sociologically* (Oxford: Blackwell, 1990) p. 10; P. L. Berger, *Invitation to Sociology: A Humanistic Introduction* (Harmondsworth: Pelican, 1966).

16. Z. Bauman, *Thinking Sociologically*, pp. 12–14.

17. R. Jenkins, *Hightown Rules: Growing Up in a Belfast Housing Estate* (Leicester: National Youth Bureau, 1982); and *Lads, Citizens and Ordinary Kids: Working Class Youth Life-styles in Belfast* (London: Routledge and Kegan Paul, 1983).

18. R. Jenkins, *Lads, Citizens and Ordinary Kids*, p. 10; and *Social Identity* (London: Routledge, 1996) pp. 11–18.

19. Z. Bauman, *Thinking Sociologically*, p. 15.

20. My favourite example is E. Schegloff, 'Sequencing in Conversational Openings', *American Anthropologist*, vol. 70 (1968) pp. 1075–95.

21. M. Weber, *Economy and Society: An Outline of Interpretive Sociology*, ed. G. Roth and C. Wittich (Berkeley: University of California Press, 1978) pp. 18–22.

22. B. Ankerloo and S. Clark (eds), *The Athlone History of Witchcraft and Magic in Europe*, vol. 4: *The Period of the Witch Trials* (London: Athlone Press, 1999); B. Ankerloo and G. Henningsen (eds), *Early Modern Witchcraft: Centres and Peripheries* (Oxford: Oxford University Press, 1990); B. P. Levack, *The Witch-Hunt in Early Modern Europe*, 2nd edn (London: Longman, 1995).

23. On witchcraft as an underground religion, see M. A. Murray, *The Witch-Cult in Western Europe* (Oxford: Oxford University Press, 1921). On the witchcraft persecutions as misogyny, see M. Hester, *Lewd Women and Wicked Witches: A Study of the Dynamics of Male Domination* (London: Routledge, 1992).

24. On the distinction between explanation and interpretation in social science, see M. Williams, *Science and Social Science*, chapters 3–5; P. Winch,

The Idea of a Social Science and its Relation to Philosophy (London: Routledge and Kegan Paul, 1958).

25. H. H. Gerth and C. Wright Mills (eds), *From Max Weber*, pp. 323–59.

26. J. H. Goldthorpe, *On Sociology*, pp. 16–17, 65–93.

Notes to Chapter Three: Society and Culture

1. J. Urry, 'Mobile Sociology', *British Journal of Sociology*, vol. 51 (2000) p. 188.

2. T. Lovell, 'Feminisms Transformed?', in B. S. Turner (ed.), *The Blackwell Companion to Social Theory*, 2nd edn (Oxford: Blackwell, 2000) p. 346.

3. It is a telling comment on the inadequacy of sociology in providing us with accounts of the self-styled élite members of the human world – see note 19 to Chapter 5, below – that the best place to start here is probably still N. Mitford (ed.), *Noblesse Oblige: An Inquiry into the Identifiable Characteristics of the English Aristocracy* (Harmondsworth: Penguin, 1956), particularly the essay by Ross.

4. In the shape of *Debrett's*, and Burke's *Peerage*, there are even guides to the bloodlines.

5. K. Fox, *The Racing Tribe: Watching the Horsewatchers* (London: Metro, 1999).

6. J. Ward, 'Telling Tales in Prison', in R. Frankenberg (ed.), *Custom and Conflict in British Society* (Manchester: Manchester University Press, 1982); M. Wright, *Making Good: Prisons, Punishment and Beyond* (London: Burnett Books, 1982) pp. 30–76. It is their microcosmic character which defines 'total institutions': E. Goffman, *Asylums: Essays on the Social Situation of Mental Patients and Other Inmates* (Harmondsworth: Pelican, 1968).

7. S. Hall *et al.*, *Policing the Crisis: Mugging the State and Law and Order* (London: Macmillan, 1976) pp. 140–50 in particular.

8. J. Raban, *God, Man and Mrs Thatcher: A Critique of Mrs Thatcher's Address to the General Assembly of the Church of Scotland* (London: Chatto and Windus, 1989) pp. 29–30.

9. J. Urry, 'Mobile Sociology', pp. 188–90; and *Sociology Beyond Societies: Mobilities for the Twenty-First Century* (London: Routledge, 2000) pp. 1–20.

10. For example, J. R. Eiser, *Social Judgment* (Milton Keynes: Open University Press, 1990) pp. 28–52, 99–122.

11. E. Durkheim, *The Rules of the Sociological Method* (New York: Free Press, 1964 [1895]) pp. 1–13; and *The Elementary Forms of the Religious Life* (London: George Allen and Unwin, 1976 [1912]) particularly pp. 415–47.

12. F. Barth, 'Introduction' to F. Barth (ed.), *Ethnic Groups and Boundaries: The Social Organisation of Culture Difference* (Oslo: Universitetsforlaget, 1969); R. Jenkins, *Rethinking Ethnicity: Arguments and Explorations* (London: Sage, 1997).

13. Meditation XVII from Donne's *Devotions upon Emergent Occasions* (1624).

14. B. S. Turner, 'Preface' to B. S. Turner (ed.), *The Blackwell Companion to Social Theory*, p. 4.

15. F. Braudel, *Civilization and Capitalism, 15th to the 18th Centuries*, vol. 2: *The Wheels of Commerce* (London: Collins, 1982); P. Hazard, *The European Mind, 1680–1715* (Harmondsworth: Penguin, 1973).

16. Times have changed since C. P. Snow's argument about the superior cultural capital of the arts and humanities: *The Two Cultures*, 2nd edn (Cambridge: Cambridge University Press, 1964). See also P. Bourdieu, *Homo Academicus* (Cambridge: Polity Press, 1988) pp. 36–69.

17. This is not a new point: T. Burns, 'Sociological Explanation', in D. Emmett and A. MacIntyre (eds), *Sociological Theory and Philosophical Analysis* (London: Macmillan, 1970) pp. 57–9.

18. On cultures of poverty: R. Cherry, 'Culture of Poverty', in P. A. O'Hara (ed.), *Encyclopedia of Political Economy*, vol. 1 (London: Routledge, 1999); C. A. Valentine, *Culture and Poverty* (Chicago: University of Chicago Press, 1968).

    On class cultures as ways of life: J. Clarke, C. Critcher and R. Johnson (eds), *Working Class Culture: Studies in History and Theory* (London: Hutchinson, 1979); R. W. Connell, *Ruling Class, Ruling Culture: Studies of Conflict, Power and Hegemony in Australian Life* (Cambridge: Cambridge University Press, 1977); M. Lamont, *Money, Morals and Manners: The Culture of the French and American Upper-Middle Classes* (Chicago: University of Chicago Press, 1992).

    On stratification as a status–attainment hierarchy of occupations and skills: D. J. Treiman and H. B. G. Ganzeboom, 'The Fourth Generation of Comparative Stratification Research', in S. R. Quah and A. Sales (eds), *The International Handbook of Sociology* (London: Sage, 2000).

On social class as competitive position in the employment, housing, and education markets: J. Rex and S. Tomlinson, *Colonial Immigrants in a British City: A Class Analysis* (London: Routledge and Kegan Paul, 1979).

On stratification as a hierarchical continuum of occupation, differential access to resources, and networks of interaction: A. Stewart, K. Prandy and R. M. Blackburn, *Social Stratification and Occupations* (London: Macmillan, 1980); R. M. Blackburn and K. Prandy, 'The Reproduction of Social Inequality', *Sociology*, vol. 31 (1997) pp. 491–510.

On class as the relationship to the means of production under capitalism: R. Crompton and J. Gubbay, *Economy and Class Structure* (London: Macmillan, 1977); S. Resnick and R. D. Wolff, *Knowledge and Class: A Marxian Critique of Political Economy* (Chicago: University of Chicago Press, 1987).

On stratification as the pattern of differential rewards accruing to rational individual decision-making in education and the labour market: J. H. Goldthorpe, *On Sociology*, pp. 161–81.

On stratification as a pattern of rewards reflecting differential individual endowments and productivity: C. Jencks *et al.*, *Inequality: A Reassessment of the Effect of Family and Schooling in America* (New York: Basic Books, 1972); R. Herrnstein and C. Murray, *The Bell Curve: Intelligence and Class Structure in American Life* (New York: Free Press, 1994).

On stratification simply as quantifiable differences in access to material resources: D. Gordon and P. Townsend (eds), *Breadline Europe: The Measurement of Poverty* (Bristol: Policy Press, 2000).

19. D. Byrne, *Social Exclusion* (Buckingham: Open University Press, 1999); B. Jordan, *A Theory of Poverty and Social Exclusion* (Cambridge: Polity Press, 1996); R. Levitas, *The Inclusive Society? Social Exclusion and New Labour* (London: Macmillan, 1998).

20. A. F. C. Wallace, *Culture and Personality*, 2nd edn (New York: Random House, 1970) pp. 24–38.

21. R. Jenkins, *Social Identity* (London: Routledge, 1996) pp. 39–67.

22. F. Braudel, *The Wheels of Commerce*; T. Crump, *The Phenomenon of Money* (London: Routledge and Kegan Paul, 1981); J. Parry and M. Bloch (eds), *Money and the Morality of Exchange* (Cambridge: Cambridge University Press, 1989); G. Simmel, *The Philosophy of Money* (London: Routledge and Kegan Paul, 1978).

23. P. Bourdieu, *Distinction: A Social Critique of the Judgement of Taste* (London: Routledge and Kegan Paul, 1984); M. Lamont, *Money, Morals and Manners.*

24. A perspective which may, paradoxically, have its roots in R. Hoggart, *The Uses of Literacy: Aspects of Working-class Life with Special Reference to Publications and Entertainments* (London: Chatto and Windus, 1957).

25. N. Elias, *The Civilizing Process: Sociogenic and Psychogenic Investigations*, revised edn (Oxford: Blackwell, 2000); P. Spierenburg, *The Broken Spell: A Cultural and Anthropological History of Preindustrial Europe* (London: Macmillan, 1991).

26. For example, J. Fiske, *Understanding Popular Culture* (London: Unwin Hyman, 1989); D. Slater, *Consumer Culture and Modernity* (Cambridge: Polity Press, 1996); P. Willis, *Common Culture: Symbolic Work at Play in the Everyday Cultures of the Young* (Buckingham: Open University Press, 1990).

27. R. Jenkins, *Rethinking Ethnicity.*

28. Ibid., pp. 9–10.

29. T. Eagleton, *The Idea of Culture* (Oxford: Blackwell, 2000) pp. 87–111.

30. M. Fortes, *Rules and the Emergence of Society*, Occasional Paper no. 39 (London: Royal Anthropological Institute, 1983); C. Lévi-Strauss, *The Elementary Structures of Kinship*, 2nd edn (Boston: Beacon Press, 1969).

31. E. B. Tylor, *Primitive Culture: Researches into the Development of Mythology, Philosophy, Religion, Language, Art and Custom* (London: J. Murray, 1871).

32. P. Bourdieu, *Outline of a Theory of Practice* (Cambridge: Cambridge University Press, 1979) p. 29.

33. G. H. Mead, *Mind, Self, and Society from the Standpoint of a Social Behaviorist* (Chicago: University of Chicago Press, 1934).

34. Among other things, I have in mind here Freud's emphasis on the formative power of early childhood experiences, and his promotion of intensive therapy as a remedy for the problems which he believed those experiences would produce.

35. G. Bateson, *Steps to an Ecology of Mind: Collected Essays in Anthropology, Psychiatry, Evolution and Epistemology* (London: Paladin, 1973).

36. R. Harré and G. Gillett, *The Discursive Mind* (Thousand Oaks: Sage, 1994).

37. R. Jenkins, *Social Identity*, pp. 51–2.

38. M. Johnson, *The Body in the Mind: The Bodily Basis of Meaning, Imagination and Reason* (Chicago: University of Chicago Press, 1987); G. Lakoff and M. Johnson, *Metaphors We Live By* (Chicago: University of Chicago Press, 1980); and *Philosophy in the Flesh: The Embodied Mind and Its*

Challenge to Western Thought (New York: Basic Books, 1999). For a different perspective on the body as a template for collectivity, see M. Douglas, *Natural Symbols: Explorations in Cosmology* (Harmondsworth: Pelican, 1973) pp. 93–112.

39. E. Durkheim, *The Rules of the Sociological Method*, pp. 47–75.

40. T. Eagleton, *The Idea of Culture*, p. 4.

41. J. Urry, *Sociology Beyond Societies*, and 'Mobile Sociology'.

42. E.g. F. Barth, *Ethnic Groups and Boundaries*; J. Boissevain, 'The Place of Non-groups in the Social Sciences', *Man* (n.s.), vol. 3 (1968) pp. 542–56; A. P. Cohen, *The Symbolic Construction of Community* (London: Harwood/ Tavistock, 1985); E. R. Leach, *Political Systems of Highland Burma: A Study of Kachin Social Structure* (London: Athlone Press, 1954).

43. See R. Jenkins, *Social Identity*, and *Rethinking Ethnicity*. For a re-formulation of the 'Thomas Rule', see A. de Swaan, *Human Societies: An Introduction* (Cambridge: Polity, 2001) pp. 30–1.

44. H. Friedmann, 'The Social Terrain: the History and Future of Sociology's Object', in J. L. Abu-Lughod (ed.), *Sociology for the Twenty-first Century: Continuities and Cutting Edges* (Chicago: University of Chicago Press, 1999).

45. T. Eagleton, *The Idea of Culture*; A. Kuper, *Culture: The Anthropologists' Account* (Cambridge, Mass.: Harvard University Press, 1999).

Notes to Chapter Four: The Human World

1. A. Schutz and T. Luckmann, *The Structures of the Life-World* (Evanston: Northwestern University Press, 1973).

2. P. Coates, *Nature: Western Attitudes since Ancient Times* (Cambridge: Polity, 1998); N. Evernden, *The Social Construction of Nature* (Baltimore: Johns Hopkins Press, 1992).

3. The ideas about identification that I draw on in this chapter are explored in detail in R. Jenkins, *Social Identity* (London: Routledge, 1996) and *Rethinking Ethnicity* (London: Sage, 1997).

4. E. Goffman, *The Presentation of Self in Everyday Life* (London: Allen Lane, 1969).

5. E. Goffman, 'The Interaction Order', *American Sociological Review*, vol. 48 (1983) pp. 1–17.

6. A. Giddens, *The Constitution of Society* (Cambridge: Polity, 1984) pp. 1–40.

7. This is a good example of the need to talk about 'the social' on occasions.

8. D. Hakken, *Cyborgs@Cyberspace? An Ethnographer Looks to the Future* (New York: Routledge, 1999) pp. 69–92. Even in accounts of the Internet which celebrate its creation of a space for fluid and playful multiplex identification, it's impossible to lose sight of the flesh and blood reality of the embodied individuals concerned. See, for example, S. Turkle, *Life on the Screen: Identity in the Age of the Internet* (London: Weidenfeld and Nicolson, 1996).

9. In addition to the sources cited in note 3 to this chapter, above, see R. Jenkins, 'Categorisation: Identity, Social Process and Epistemology', *Current Sociology*, vol. 48 (2000) no. 3, pp. 7–25.

10. G. H. Mead, *Mind, Self, and Society from the Standpoint of a Social Behaviorist* (Chicago: University of Chicago Press, 1934) pp. 135–226.

11. For an historical and ethnographic account of these unofficial networks in Sheffield, see G. Armstrong, *Football Hooligans: Knowing the Score* (Oxford: Berg, 1998).

12. J. Elster, *Ulysses and the Sirens: Studies in Rationality and Irrationality* (Cambridge: Cambridge University Press, 1979); J. H. Goldthorpe, *On Sociology: Numbers, Narratives and the Integration of Research and Theory* (Oxford: Oxford University Press, 2000) pp. 94–136.

13. P. L. Berger and T. Luckmann, *The Social Construction of Reality* (London: Allen Lane, 1967), pp. 70–85; P. Bourdieu, *The Logic of Practice* (Cambridge: Polity Press, 1990) pp. 52–97.

14. L. Althusser, *Lenin and Philosophy, and Other Essays* (London: Verso, 1971) especially pp. 127–86; A. Giddens, *The Constitution of Society*, pp. 162–226.

15. I. Craib, *Experiencing Identity* (London: Sage, 1998); A. Giddens, *The Constitution of Society*, pp. 41–109; K. Woodward, 'Concepts of Identity and Difference', in K. Woodward (ed.), *Identity and Difference* (London: Sage, 1997) pp. 42–6.

16. E. Durkheim, *The Rules of the Sociological Method* (New York: Free Press, 1964 [1895]) pp. 4–6; M. Weber, *Economy and Society: An Outline of Interpretive Sociology*, ed. G. Roth and C. Wittich (Berkeley: University of California Press, 1978) pp. 4–26.

17. R. Harré (ed.), *The Social Construction of Emotions* (Oxford: Blackwell, 1986); C. A. Lutz and G. M. White, 'The Anthropology of Emotions', *Annual Review of Anthropology*, vol. 15 (1986) pp. 405–36. This is a

further example of the impossibility of avoiding completely words such as 'social' and 'cultural'.

18. Entertainingly enough, a good example of this is me writing this passage: I am undoubtedly motivated to do so, at least in part, by the existence of the concept 'structure' . . . Ho hum.

19. M. Weber, *Economy and Society*, pp. 24–6.

20. M. G. Smith, *Government in Zazzau, 1800–1950* (London: Oxford University Press, 1960) pp. 15–33.

21. S. J. Gould, *Wonderful Life: The Burgess Shale and the Nature of History* (London: Hutchinson Radius, 1989). For other perspectives on the same issues, see, *inter alia*, J. Weiner, *The Beak of the Finch: A Story of Evolution in Our Time* (New York: Knopf, 1994); E. O. Wilson, *The Diversity of Life* (Cambridge, Mass.: Belknap Press, 1992).

22. H. H. Gerth and C. Wright Mills (eds), *From Max Weber: Essays in Sociology* (London: Routledge and Kegan Paul, 1948) pp. 323–59.

23. R. Jenkins, 'Disenchantment, Enchantment and Re-enchantment: Max Weber at the Millennium', *Max Weber Studies*, vol. 1 (2000) pp. 11–32.

24. P. L. Berger and T. Luckmann, *The Social Construction of Reality*, pp. 110–46.

25. K. H. Wolff (ed.), *The Sociology of Georg Simmel* (New York: Free Press, 1950) Part Two: 'Quantitative Aspects of the Group'.

26. H. Bergson, *Time and Free Will* (London: Swann Sonnenschein, 1910); E. Husserl, *The Phenomenology of Internal Time Consciousness* (The Hague: Martinus Nijhoff, 1964).

27. G. H. Mead, *The Philosophy of the Present*, ed. A. E. Murphy (Chicago: University of Chicago Press, 1980) pp. 1–32.

Notes to Chapter Five: Exploring the Human World

1. This expression derives from Lakoff and Johnson's advocacy of 'empirically responsible philosophy', in G. Lakoff and M. Johnson, *Philosophy in the Flesh: The Embodied Mind and Its Challenge to Western Thought* (New York: Basic Books, 1999) pp. 551–68.

2. This is a reference to Karl Popper's philosophy of science: for a review, see M. Williams, *Science and Social Science: An Introduction* (London: Routledge, 2000) pp. 35–9. For some implications of this position, see

J. H. Goldthorpe, *On Sociology: Numbers, Narratives and the Integration of Research into Theory* (Oxford: Oxford University Press, 2000) pp. 137–60.

3. This argument can be taken further, and categorisation understood as an innate attribute of all 'neural beings': G. Lakoff and M. Johnson, *Philosophy in the Flesh*, pp. 17–20. This, however, stretches the notion of categorisation beyond what I have in mind: R. Jenkins, 'Categorisation: Identity, Social Process and Epistemology', *Current Sociology*, vol. 48 (2000) no. 3, pp. 7–25.

4. M. Castells, *The Information Age: Economy, Society and Culture*, vol. 1: *The Rise of the Network Society* (Malden, Mass.: Blackwell, 1996) pp. 358–64.

5. For a good and even-handed discussion of the relationship between 'natural' science and 'social' science, see M. Williams, *Science and Social Science*.

6. E.g. D. Silverman, 'Telling Convincing Stories: a Plea for Cautious Positivism in Case-Studies', in B. Glassner and J. D. Moreno (eds), *The Quantitative–Qualitative Distinction in the Social Sciences* (The Hague: Kluwer, 1989). See also the discussion in A. Bryman, *Social Research Methods* (Oxford: Oxford University Press, 2001) pp. 429–31.

7. The origins of the positions I am implicitly criticising here are to be found in critiques of abstract empiricism and the like which were, at the time, absolutely vital if sociology was to survive as a discipline actively engaged with the human world.

8. P. L. Berger and T. Luckmann, *The Social Construction of Reality* (London: Allen Lane, 1967); J. R. Searle, *The Construction of Social Reality* (London: Allen Lane, 1995); W. I. Thomas, 'The Relation of Research to the Social Process', in M. Janowitz (ed.), *W. I. Thomas on Social Organization and Social Personality* (Chicago: University of Chicago Press, 1966). See also: K. Gergen, *An Invitation to Social Construction* (Thousand Oaks: Sage, 1999), and *Social Construction in Context* (Thousand Oaks: Sage, 2001).

9. This comes from Part One of *The German Ideology* (1845–6), the section on 'Ruling Class and Ruling Ideas'.

10. J. Clifford and G. E. Marcus (eds), *Writing Culture: The Poetics and Politics of Ethnography* (Berkeley: University of California Press, 1986); J. Clifford, *The Predicament of Culture: Twentieth-Century Ethnography, Literature and Art* (Cambridge, Mass.: Harvard University Press, 1988).

11. T. Docherty, 'Postmodernism: an Introduction', in T. Docherty (ed.), *Postmodernism: A Reader* (Hemel Hempstead: Harvester Wheatsheaf, 1993) pp. 5–14, 22–7.

12. See M. Williams, *Problems of Knowledge: A Critical Introduction to Epistemology* (Oxford: Oxford University Press, 2001).

13. For different sociological sides of this particular argument in Britain, see J. S. La Fontaine, *Speak of the Devil: Tales of Satanic Abuse in Contemporary England* (Cambridge: Cambridge University Press, 1998); and S. Scott, *The Politics and Experience of Ritual Abuse: Beyond Disbelief* (Buckingham: Open University Press, 2001).

14. A. Giddens, *Modernity and Self-Identity: Self and Society in the Late Modern Age* (Cambridge: Polity Press, 1991). For critiques on empirical grounds, see R. Jenkins, *Social Identity* (London: Routledge, 1996) pp. 9–10; and B. S. Turner, 'An Outline of a General Sociology of the Body', in B. S. Turner (ed.), *The Blackwell Companion to Social Theory*, 2nd edn (Oxford: Blackwell, 2000) p. 490.

15. See note 2 to this chapter, above.

16. T. S. Kuhn, *The Structure of Scientific Revolutions*, 2nd edn (Chicago: University of Chicago Press, 1970); I. Lakatos and A. Musgrave (eds), *Criticism and the Growth of Knowledge* (Cambridge: Cambridge University Press, 1970).

17. G. Ryle, *The Concept of Mind* (London: Hutchinson, 1949).

18. Z. Bauman, *Thinking Sociologically* (Oxford: Blackwell, 1990) p. 12.

19. See G. Moyser and M. Wagstaffe (eds), *Research Methods for Elite Studies* (London: Allen and Unwin, 1987).

20. J. H. Goldthorpe, *On Sociology*, pp. 65–93.

21. C. Wright Mills, *The Sociological Imagination* (New York: Oxford University Press, 1959) p. 96.

22. A. Bryman, *Quantity and Quality in Social Research* (London: Unwin Hyman, 1988), and *Social Research Methods*, pp. 427–57.

23. This is discussed in A. Bryman, *Quantity and Quality in Social Research*, pp. 38–42.

24. R. Jenkins, *Social Identity* (London: Routledge, 1996) pp. 51–2.

25. A. Giddens, *Social Theory and Modern Sociology* (Cambridge: Polity Press, 1987) pp. 20–1.

26. The original formulations are 'Man in Society' and 'Society in Man', in P. Berger, *Invitation to Sociology: A Humanistic Introduction* (Harmondsworth: Pelican, 1966).

Notes to Chapter Six: The Human World and the Natural World

1. This could be approached from a different angle, in that positivism and realism are based on epistemological and methodological assumptions that there is continuity between humans and 'nature'. This means that in principle the same or similar procedures are appropriate to their investigation. See M. Williams, *Science and Social Science: An Introduction* (London: Routledge, 2000) pp. 47–51.

2. The 'hegemony of social constructionism' is discussed in T. Lovell, 'Feminisms of the Second Wave', in B. S. Turner (ed.), *The Blackwell Companion to Social Theory*, 2nd edn (Oxford: Blackwell, 2000) pp. 305–8. Lovell, somewhat ironically, equates being a 'good sociologist' with denying 'any role to biology' (p. 311). For a balanced introduction to the muddles into which we have talked ourselves over biology, sex and gender, see L. Segal, *Why Feminism? Gender, Psychology and Politics* (Cambridge: Polity Press, 1999). For an understanding of disability which downplays organic embodiment, see C. Barnes, G. Mercer and T. Shakespeare, *Exploring Disability: A Sociological Introduction* (Cambridge: Polity Press, 1999) pp. 10–38.

3. T. Eagleton, *The Idea of Culture* (Oxford: Blackwell, 2000) p. 88.

4. E.g. B. Adam, *Timescapes of Modernity: The Environment and Invisible Hazards* (London: Routledge, 1998); U. Beck, *Risk Society: Towards a New Modernity* (London: Sage, 1992); D. Goldblatt, *Social Theory and the Environment* (Cambridge: Polity Press, 1996); P. MacNaghten and J. Urry, 'Towards a Sociology of Nature', *Sociology*, vol. 29 (1995) pp. 203–20; S. Yearley, *Sociology, Environmentalism, Globalization: Reinventing the Globe* (London: Sage, 1996).

5. M. S. Archer, *Being Human: The Problem of Agency* (Cambridge: Cambridge University Press, 2000); M. Carrithers, *Why Humans Have Cultures: Explaining Anthropology and Social Diversity* (Oxford: Oxford University Press, 1992); A. de Swaan, *Human Societies: An Introduction* (Cambridge: Polity Press, 2001); A. Kuper, *The Chosen Primate: Human Nature and Cultural Diversity* (Cambridge, Mass.: Harvard University Press, 1996); W. G. Runciman, *A Treatise on Social Theory*, vol. II: *Substantive Social Theory* (Cambridge: Cambridge University Press, 1989) pp. 37–48; B. S. Turner and C. Rojek, *Society and Culture: Principles of Scarcity and Solidarity* (London: Sage, 2001).

6. For a view of this process in the very long term, and from a perspective which is outside the axiomatic anthropocentric cosmology, see N. Eldredge, *Dominion* (Berkeley: University of California Press, 1997).

7. See P. Coates, *Nature: Western Attitudes since Ancient Times* (Cambridge: Polity, 1998); N. Evernden, *The Social Construction of Nature* (Baltimore: Johns Hopkins Press, 1992).

8. See the papers and discussions in *Nature*, vol. 409, no. 6822 (15 February 2001), and *Science*, vol. 291, no. 5507 (16 February 2001).

9. M. Carrithers, *Why Humans Have Cultures*.

10. Summarised, as the heart of a powerful ethical argument, in M. Ignatieff, *The Needs of Strangers* (London: Chatto and Windus, 1984).

11. Marx's life's work was imbued by a consistent and powerful vision of human needs and nature, the perversion and denial of which by capitalism was the wellspring of his politics. This begins with the discussion of the humanity of labour and production, in *The Economic and Philosophical Manuscripts* (1844), and continues all the way through to the discussion of the working day, and the effects of mechanisation, in chapters X and XV of *Capital*, vol. 1 (first published in 1867).

12. S. Freud, *The Essentials of Psycho-Analysis*, ed. A. Freud (Harmondsworth: Penguin, 1986) pp. 191–268.

13. A. Maslow, 'A Theory of Human Motivation', *Psychological Review*, vol. 50 (1943) pp. 370–96.

14. For example, the papers collected in W. Beck, L. van der Maesen and A. Walker (eds), *The Social Quality of Europe* (The Hague: Kluwer, 1997).

15. L. Doyal and I. Gough, *A Theory of Human Need* (Basingstoke: Macmillan, 1991).

16. A. de Swaan, *Human Societies*.

17. A representative example of a straight social-constructionist approach to embodiment is C. Shilling, *The Body and Social Theory* (London: Sage, 1993). An interesting alternative approach to the human condition, stressing the intrinsic vulnerability of the body, and positing collective solidarity as a solution, is B. S. Turner and C. Rojek, *Society and Culture*.

18. S. J. Gould, *The Mismeasure of Man*, revised and expanded edition (New York: Norton, 1996); P. V. Tobias, 'Race', in A. Kuper and J. Kuper (eds), *The Social Science Encyclopedia*, 2nd edn (London: Routledge, 1996).

19. F. Dikötter (ed.), *The Construction of Racial Identities in China and Japan* (London: Hurst, 1997); V. G. Kiernan, *The Lords of Human Kind: Black Man, Yellow Man, and White Man in an Age of Empire* (London: Cresset, 1988 [1969]); R. Miles, *Racism* (London: Routledge, 1989) pp. 11–40; J. Rex, *Race and Ethnicity* (Milton Keynes: Open University Press, 1986) pp. 38–58.

20. See, for example, M. Burleigh and W. Wippermann, *The Racial State: Germany, 1933–1945* (Cambridge: Cambridge University Press, 1991).

21. C. Barnes, G. Mercer and T. Shakespeare, *Exploring Disability: A Sociological Introduction* (Cambridge: Polity Press, 1999) pp. 10–38; B. Ingstad and S. R. Whyte, 'Disability and Culture: An Overview', in B. Ingstad and S. R. Whyte (eds), *Disability and Culture* (Berkeley: University of California Press, 1995).

22. M. Oliver, *The Politics of Disablement* (London: Macmillan, 1990); D. A. Stone, *The Disabled State* (London: Macmillan, 1984).

23. On the facts of sexual dimorphism, see J. M. Tanner, 'Human Growth and Development', in S. Jones, R. Martin and D. Pilbeam (eds), *The Cambridge Encyclopedia of Human Evolution* (Cambridge: Cambridge University Press, 1992) pp. 101–3.

24. On the possible economic and familial implications of this in an evolutionary perspective, see N. Eldredge, *Dominion*, pp. 104–15.

25. Three issues which come to mind are: (i) the contribution of hunter-gathering, the mode of subsistence of humanity for most of its existence, to the stubborn persistence of gendered divisions of space, mobility and labour; (ii) the question of why, if differential physical power is important, we also have the massive symbolic over-reinforcement of gender differentiation; and (iii) the complexities of the relationship between sexual partnership between individuals, and parenthood, particularly motherhood.

26. F. Engels, *The Origin of the Family, Private Property and the State*, first published in 1884, is available in a variety of editions.

27. See T. Lovell, 'Feminisms Transformed?', in B. S. Turner (ed.), *The Blackwell Companion to Social Theory*, pp. 333–42.

28. R. Jenkins, *Social Identity* (London: Routledge, 1996) pp. 80–9.

29. See Y. L. Espiritu, *Asian American Panethnicity: Bridging Institutions and Identities* (Philadelphia: Temple University Press, 1992); M. Omi and H. Wynant, *Racial Formation in the United States: From the 1960s to the*

1980s (New York: Routledge and Kegan Paul, 1986); B. Ringer, *'We the People and Others: Duality and America's Treatment of Its Racial Minorities* (New York: Tavistock, 1983).

30. For a range of perspectives, see L. Barton and M. Oliver (eds), *Disability Studies: Past, Present and Future* (Leeds: Disability Press, 1997) particularly the chapters by Chappell, Walmsley, Campbell, Corbett, Borsay, Barton, and Oliver and Zarb.

31. H. Bradley, *Fractured Identities: Changing Patterns of Inequality* (Cambridge: Polity Press, 1996); B. Skeggs, *Formations of Class and Gender* (London: Sage, 1997); S. Walby, *Theorizing Patriarchy* (Oxford: Blackwell, 1990).

32. B. S. Turner and C. Rojek, *Society and Culture*; B. S. Turner, 'An Outline of a General Sociology of the Body', in B. S. Turner (ed.), *The Blackwell Companion to Social Theory*.

33. See M. Harris, *Culture, People, Nature: An Introduction to General Anthropology*, 7th edn (New York: Addison-Wesley, 1997); T. Ingold (ed.), *Companion Encyclopedia of Anthropology: Humanity, Culture and Social Life* (London: Routledge, 1994), chapters by Odling-Smee, Ellen, and Rapoport.

34. F. Braudel, *Civilization and Capitalism, 15th to the 18th Centuries*, vol. 1: *The Structures of Everyday Life* (London: Collins, 1981) pp. 31–103.

35. See P. Coates, *Nature*; N. Evenden, *The Social Construction of Nature*.

36. See N. Eldredge, *Dominion*.

37. See, for example, G. D. Flood (ed.), *Mapping Invisible Worlds* (Edinburgh: Edinburgh University Press, 1993); C. P. MacCormack and M. Strathern (eds), *Nature, Culture and Gender* (Cambridge: Cambridge University Press, 1980).

38. M. S. Archer, *Being Human*; B. S. Turner and C. Rojek, *Society and Culture*.

39. F. J. Gil-White, 'How Thick is Blood? The plot thickens . . . : if ethnic actors are primordialists, what remains of the circumstantialist/primordialist controversy?', *Ethnic and Racial Studies*, vol. 22 (1999) pp. 789–820; R. Jenkins, *Rethinking Ethnicity: Arguments and Explorations* (London: Sage, 1997) pp. 44–8.

Notes to Chapter Seven: Why Sociology Matters

1. T. Burns, 'Sociological Explanation', in D. Emmett and A. MacIntyre (eds), *Sociological Theory and Philosophical Analysis* (London: Macmillan, 1970) p. 72.

2. See note 1 to Chapter 5, above.

3. See note 11 to Chapter 1, above.

4. J. Urry, *Sociology Beyond Societies: Mobilities for the Twenty-First Century* (London: Routledge, 2000).

5. J. Henry, *Culture Against Man* (Harmondsworth: Penguin, 1972).

6. A. MacIntyre, *After Virtue: A Study in Moral Theory*, 2nd edn (London: Duckworth, 1985); and *Dependable Rational Animals: Why Human Beings Need the Virtues* (London: Duckworth, 1999).

7. B. S. Turner and C. Rojek, *Society and Culture: Principles of Scarcity and Solidarity* (London: Sage, 2001).

8. G. Ritzer, *Enchanting a Disenchanted World: Revolutionizing the Means of Consumption* (Thousand Oaks: Pine Forge, 1999).

9. Z. Bauman, *In Search of Politics* (Cambridge: Polity Press, 2001); *Liquid Modernity* (Cambridge: Polity Press, 2000) pp. 168–201; and *Community: Seeking Safety in an Insecure World* (Cambridge: Polity Press, 2001).

10. R. Fevre, *The Demoralization of Western Culture: Social Theory and the Dilemmas of Modern Living* (London: Continuum, 2000).

11. S. Andreski, *Social Sciences as Sorcery* (London: André Deutsch, 1972) pp. 59–93; H. S. Becker, *Writing for Social Scientists* (Chicago: University of Chicago Press, 1986); C. Wright Mills, *The Sociological Imagination* (New York: Oxford University Press, 1959) pp. 25–7, 217–22.

12. On Freud, see F. Crews (ed.), *Unauthorized Freud: Doubters Confront a Legend* (New York: Penguin, 1998); J. M. Masson, *The Assault on Truth: Freud's Suppression of the Seduction Theory*, 2nd edn (New York: Harper, 1992). On Burt, see R. B. Joynson, *The Burt Affair* (London: Routledge, 1989); N. J. Mackintosh (ed.), *Cyril Burt: Fraud or Framed?* (Oxford: Oxford University Press, 1995).

13. See note 13 to Chapter 5, above.

14. The sociology of culture – and particularly the study of consumption – is perhaps the most obvious example here. However, other examples of sociological work which cheerfully resist the discipline's miserabilist tendencies can be found in studies of childhood, community, religion, science, and sexuality.

15. D. E. Smith, 'From Women's Standpoint to a Sociology for People', in J. L. Abu-Lughod (ed.), *Sociology for the Twenty-first Century: Continuities and Cutting Edges* (Chicago: University of Chicago Press, 1999).

16. A. Giddens, *Social Theory and Modern Sociology* (Cambridge: Polity Press, 1987) pp. 20–1.

Index